MARCIA REYNOLDS

COACH THE PERSON,

NOT THE PROBLEM

A Guide to Using
Reflective
Inquiry

BK

Berrett–Koehler Publishers, Inc.

Berrett-Koehler Publishers, Inc.
1333 Broadway, Suite 1000
Oakland, CA 94612-1921
Tel: (510) 817-2277
Fax: (510) 817-2278
www.bkconnection.com

ORDERING INFORMATION

Quantity sales. Special discounts are available on quantity purchases by corporations, associations, and others. For details, contact the "Special Sales Department" at the Berrett-Koehler address above.

Individual sales. Berrett-Koehler publications are available through most bookstores. They can also be ordered directly from Berrett-Koehler: Tel: (800) 929-2929; Fax: (802) 864-7626; www.bkconnection.com.

Orders for college textbook / course adoption use. Please contact Berrett-Koehler: Tel: (800) 929-2929; Fax: (802) 864-7626.

Distributed to the U.S. trade and internationally by Penguin Random House Publisher Services.

Berrett-Koehler and the BK logo are registered trademarks of Berrett-Koehler Publishers, Inc.

Printed in Canada.

Berrett-Koehler books are printed on long-lasting acid-free paper. When it is available, we choose paper that has been manufactured by environmentally responsible processes. These may include using trees grown in sustainable forests, incorporating recycled paper, minimizing chlorine in bleaching, or recycling the energy produced at the paper mill.

Library of Congress Cataloging-in-Publication Data

Names: Reynolds, Marcia, author.
Title: Coach the person, not the problem : a guide to using reflective inquiry / Marcia Reynolds.
Description: First edition. | Oakland, CA : Berrett-Koehler Publishers, 2020. | Includes bibliographical references and index.
Identifiers: LCCN 2019054216 | ISBN 9781523087839 (paperback) | ISBN 9781523087846 (pdf) | ISBN 9781523087853 (epub)
Subjects: LCSH: Personal coaching. | Counselor and client.
Classification: LCC BF637.P36 R49 2020 | DDC 158.3--dc23
LC record available at https://lccn.loc.gov/2019054216

First Edition
25 24 23 22 21 20   10 9 8 7 6 5 4 3 2

Copyediting: PeopleSpeak
Book design and composition: Marin Bookworks
Cover design: Irene Morris

COACH THE
PERSON,
NOT THE PROBLEM

To my parents, who never gave up on me
no matter what problems I created.

CONTENTS

ASKING QUESTIONS IS NOT THE SAME AS INQUIRY

MANY POPULAR BOOKS, leadership actions, and coaching guidelines outline rules for asking good questions. Common rules include ask open questions; start with what, when, where, how, and who; and avoid why questions.

These suggestions are misleading.

Coaches and leaders spend more time trying to remember the questions they're supposed to ask than paying attention to the person they are coaching. [1] They end up "checklist coaching" to ensure their questions follow the model they were taught in coaching school or a leadership workshop, which is more frustrating for the client than helpful.

Not only do coaches spend more time in their own heads than listening, they make coaching more complex than it should be. They don't realize that being present and using reflective statements such as summarizing, paraphrasing, and drawing distinctions can be more powerful—and easier—than seeking the magical question. When a coach asks a question *after* providing a reflection, the question is more likely to arise out of curiosity, not memory. At this point, even a closed question can lead to a breakthrough in thinking.

Coaching should be a process of *inquiry*, not a series of questions. The intent of *inquiry* is not to find solutions but to provoke critical thinking about our own thoughts. Inquiry helps the people being coached discern gaps in their logic, evaluate their beliefs, and clarify fears and desires affecting their choices. Solutions emerge when thoughts are rearranged and expanded.

Statements that prompt us to look inside our brains are *reflective*. They trigger reflection. Reflective statements include recapping, labeling, using metaphors, identifying key or conflicting points, and recognizing emotional shifts. *Inquiry* combines questions with reflective statements.

> Questions seek answers;
> inquiry provokes insight.

When using reflective statements in coaching, clients hear their words, see how their beliefs form their perceptions, and face the emotions they are expressing. Then, a follow-up question that either confirms (Is this true for you?) or prompts exploration (when the coach is curious about what, when, where, how, or who) provokes clients to look into their thoughts.

> Reflective statements + questions =
> reflective inquiry.

Adding reflective statements to questions makes coaching feel more natural and effortless. You don't have to worry about formulating the breakthrough question.

> Pairing reflective statements with questions frees the coach of the weight of finding the perfect/best/right question.

On the other hand, some professionals who call themselves coaches ask questions for the purpose of determining what advice to give. They criticize the International Coaching Federation (ICF), formerly known as the International Coach Federation, for rigidly imposing requirements around question asking. A Harvard psychology professor told me she wasn't an ICF credentialed coach because her high-level executive clients didn't want her to ask about how they were feeling. "It's a waste of time to question their thoughts and emotions," she said. "They want my expertise. They are clueless and need advice or a kick in the butt." It's possible that's what her clients need, but that isn't coaching. It's face-slapping mentoring.

I fear the loss of coaching as a distinct profession when the word *coaching* is diluted by people preferring to give advice. Coaching is an effective technology for helping people quickly reframe, shift perspective, and redefine themselves and their situations. Coaches act as *thinking partners* for people who are stuck inside their stories and perceptions. They help clients think more broadly for themselves, beyond their blinding fears, inherited beliefs, and half-baked assumptions that limit possible actions. As a result of this new perspective, clients discover new solutions, take action on solutions they had avoided, and commit to long-term behavioral changes more often than when they are told what to do.

The goal of coaching is to get clients to stop and question the thoughts and behaviors that limit their perspective so they can see a new way forward to achieve their desires. Reflective practices provide an instant replay for clients to observe themselves telling their stories. The questions then help clients identify the beliefs and behavioral patterns they are using. They see for themselves what patterns are ineffective, even damaging. If done with patience and respect, it's likely your clients will clearly see what they need to do without your brilliant advice.

The use of reflective inquiry as a powerful learning technology has been around for over one hundred years. I'll explain the origins of reflective inquiry in part I.

COACHING SHOULDN'T BE SO HARD

Using reflective inquiry with a caring and appreciative presence creates a connection where clients feel safe to critically explore how they think. Clients don't feel pressured to explore their blocks more deeply; they naturally go deeper. Hearing their own words prompts them to willingly dissect the meaning of their statements. They admit when their words are defensive rationalizations for behavior that doesn't align with their core values and desires.

When you coach as a thinking partner instead of an expert, your job is to *catch and return* what you are given by the client. You don't have to concoct a masterful question. You don't need to figure out if what you want to say is intuition or a blatant projection of your own needs. You don't have to have all the answers. You are a good coach if you share what you hear and see and maybe offer what you sense is happening with no attachment to being right.

You will probably ask a question after you share what you heard, saw, and sensed, but the question will come out of your reflection, not your overused "good questions" list.

When I teach these techniques, coaches from around the world say things like this:

"Thank you. You freed me from the tyranny of asking the perfect question."

"I feel so much lighter after watching you coach."

"You showed me how to have fun with my coaching."

"Yes! Be present, be the mirror, and lighten up!"

This book will show how anyone wanting to use a coaching approach in conversations can use reflective inquiry to be more present and effective. The methods and examples will demonstrate how to achieve memorable and meaningful results whether you are a professional coach or a leader, parent, teacher, or friend using a coaching approach in your conversations.

WHAT'S IN THIS BOOK

In part I, I will clarify what practices are needed to have a conversation focused on coaching the person to better think through dilemmas. Since the word *coaching* has been applied to a range of activities, I want us to begin with a common understanding of the framework we will be exploring.

Chapter 1 explains why this method of coaching—reflective inquiry—is so powerful in changing minds and leading to long-term behavioral change. I'll describe how reflective inquiry maps to the brain science around insight formation, an important element in learning, and how coaching supports clients to explore their thinking in a way they can't do themselves.

The first chapter also takes a look at the ideal moments to put on a coaching hat. Coaching isn't intended to be used in all situations. You will annoy your employees, friends, and spouse if you're always a coach. You need good reason and sometimes, permission. You'll find a list of scenarios considered good opportunities for coaching.

Chapter 2 explores five beliefs that have thrown the intention of coaching offtrack. I will explain each one, why all of them are true only some of the time, and how they limit the effectiveness of coaching when interpreted as rigid rules. I will also offer an alternative opinion for each belief with examples showing how it works within the context of the coaching relationship.

Part II, the heart of this book, will give you an understanding of and ways to implement the five essential practices for breakthrough coaching:

1. Focus—coaching the person, not the problem
2. Active Replay—playing back the pivotal pieces for review
3. Brain Hacking—finding the treasures in the box
4. Goaltending—staying the course
5. New and Next—coaxing insights and commitments

Coaching mastery isn't just about improving skills; mastery also requires that you quickly catch internal disruptions and shift back to being fully present with your clients. Part III explains and gives exercises for cultivating the three mental habits needed to master the practices of reflective inquiry:

1. Align your brain.
2. Receive (don't just listen).
3. Catch and release judgment.

I have had the opportunity to demonstrate to thousands of coaches worldwide both the essential practices and mental habits. Either they thank me for what they learned or they thank me for what I helped them remember because they knew it all along.

When I teach these practices to leaders, they realize their primary excuse for not coaching—*I don't have time*—is based in their fear that they can't coach effectively. They have probably tried and failed as they grappled to find good questions. This book gives leaders a coaching approach that reduces their fears when they discover easy steps to implement for quick and more binding results.

Once leaders work with reflective inquiry, they discover it is the best way to prompt a strong shift in perspective and action in a short time. Additionally, the conversations are creative and meaningful as well as productive, inspiring others to learn and grow. Employees feel seen, heard, and valued—the key to increasing engagement, productivity, and excitement around new ideas.

People who have experienced good coaching say it changed their lives. The essence of coaching isn't based in problem-solving or performance improvement. Those committed to using reflective inquiry are change agents who actively recharge the human spirit. At times when events at work and in the world dampen the spirit, coaching brightens the path.

PART I

WHAT IS A COACHING CONVERSATION?

*Coaching is so much more
than asking good questions.*

—MARCIA REYNOLDS

THE FOUNDING MEMBERS of the International Coaching Federation asked the question, "What makes coaching different from therapy and consulting?" The ICF definition of coaching emerged from this conversation:

> Coaching is partnering with clients in a thought-provoking and creative process that inspires them to maximize their personal and professional potential.[1]

The key word in the definition is *partnering.* Coaches do not act as experts or analysts even when they have relevant experience and education. Coaches are essentially thinking partners focused on helping clients use their creativity and resources to see beyond their blocks and solve their own problems.

The passion and commitment that fuels the continual growth of coaching is grounded in the coaching experience for both coach and client. For me—when I don't give in to my urge to advise—nothing is more fulfilling than seeing my clients laugh at themselves when they realize they've been clinging to an outdated belief. I love the spark in their eyes when they discover the answer to their problems on their own. They feel relief and gratitude when they recognize they won't be hurting anyone by following their dreams. When I feel the courage in my clients bubble up, it's my pleasure to help them put their desires into motion.

People need to feel seen, heard, and valued to have the desire to grow. In this space, their creative brains are activated. They feel safe enough to explore their own thinking and actions. Surfacing their judgments and fears may feel uncomfortable, but when clients see how to move beyond these blocks, they feel empowered.

Although many gurus have been cited as saying people are naturally creative, resourceful, and whole, this concept was first seen in the work of psychologist Alfred Adler. Adler asked us to believe in the power people feel when realizing their potential. He said, "Man knows much more than he understands."[2]

In breaking away from the ideas of his teacher Sigmund Freud, Adler said we do not have to plumb the depths of one's psychological history to help normal people progress. If, as Adler said, "we determine ourselves by the meanings we give to situations," then changing or expanding the meaning opens new possibilities to define ourselves and our actions.[3]

Adler's perspective spawned many modern therapies. The regard Adler held for the masses is a foundational concept for coaching. For people who are not seeking therapy but know they will benefit from exploring how they think when unsure of decisions or actions, coaching fills the gap.

WHERE DOES THE TERM *REFLECTIVE INQUIRY* COME FROM?

We owe gratitude to Adler for defining the coaching relationship. Yet even though coaching may be similar to cognitive behavioral therapies and question-based relationship consulting, the actual practice of coaching maps more directly to John Dewey's learning theory than to a therapeutic or commercial approach.

In 1910, Dewey defined the practice of *reflective inquiry* in his classic book, *How We Think*.[4] As an educational reformer, Dewey wanted to change the practice of dumping information into students' brains and then testing their memorization skills. He wasn't just advocating for teachers to ask more questions. He defined methods of inquiry that would prompt students to doubt what they thought they knew so they were open to expansive learning.

Dewey felt that combining the tools that provoke critical thinking with Socratic questioning would prompt students to go inward to give their thoughts serious consideration. They would then be able to distinguish what they know from what they don't know, confirm or negate a stated belief, and substantiate the value of a fear or doubt. He said that metaphorically, reflective inquiry enables us to climb a tree in our minds.[5] We gain a wider view to see connections and faults in our thinking to better assess what to do next.

WATCHING THE MOVIE FROM THE TOP OF THE TREE

Reflective inquiry includes statements that hold up a mirror to our thoughts and beliefs to provoke evaluation. The practice of mirroring, or what I call *active replay*, includes when the coach summarizes, paraphrases, acknowledges key phrases, and shares the emotions and gestures clients express. Clients then expand on the meaning of their words with explanations or corrections. They may drop into silence, shifting their eyes up, down, or sideways as they look into their thoughts. Coaches will often pause to let their clients think. If the pause is unbearably long, the coach might offer a reflection and question such as "It looks like you are considering something. What is coming up for you now?"

When coaches use reflective statements, people hear their words, see how their beliefs form their perceptions, and face the emotions they are expressing. Then, when coaches follow up with a confirming question ("Is this what you believe?") or exploratory question ("What is causing your hesitation?"), clients are prompted to stop and examine their thinking.

> We use *reflective statements* plus questions to trigger people to *reflect* on how they think.

Coaching behaviors include *noticing* energy shifts, tone of voice, pace of speech, inflection, and behaviors. Coaches *play back* clients' beliefs and assumptions to examine their verity and limitations. They *summarize* complex outcomes and possibilities, offering the statements to clients to accept or alter. They *offer observations* when clients show resistance. They *reflect progress* to reinforce movement and growth. The goal of offering reflective statements is not to lead clients in a specific direction but to help them clarify and evaluate their thoughts.

By using reflective practices, coaches encourage clients to think about what they said and expressed. The coach accepts the client's responses, even if the client gets defensive or uncomfortable. Giving clients a judgment-free space to process the coaching observations is critical to their progress.

John Dewey may not have been successful at transforming our educational systems, but his gift of defining how to grow people's minds can be seen in the actions of trained coaches.

COACHING ISN'T RAH-RAH

Most people I know like the idea of having someone act as a sounding board when they feel stuck trying to think through a dilemma. Talking about a problem can help people look at how their thoughts help or hinder their goal achievement. They don't want nonspecific encouragement. "You can do it" statements feel patronizing, especially to the high achiever.

In fact, good coaching isn't always comfortable. Learning often happens in a moment of awkward uncertainty—when we come to doubt the beliefs and assumptions that underlie our choices. Dewey also acknowledged the discomfort that accompanies doubt as inherent in the process of learning. A surprising fact, disruptive reflection, or incisive question is needed to break down what we think we know. Then, we are open to learning. The breakdown doesn't always feel good. Yet over time, we usually are grateful for the insights we gain.

For example, I had a boss who had this uncanny ability to read me. He knew what drove me, what I desperately wanted, and what barriers my own brain created that got in my way. His questions broke through the walls in my mind so I could see my blind spots. My realizations were often painful, but I knew what I had to do differently.

Once, when I was on a rampage about the incompetency of my peers and the overload of work I then had to do, he said, "It seems that everyone disappoints you." As I paused to think about his observation, he added, "Will anyone ever be good enough for you?" There was nothing left for me to say.

Back at my desk, I wondered if I had always focused on other people's flaws. I saw how this pattern had hurt my personal relationships for years. With one reflection plus one question, he made me face how I was playing out this pattern at work. I would never see my work relationships the same again.

His observation and question made me stop and question my thinking, which was terribly uncomfortable. In the midst of this discomfort, I became more conscious of how I distanced myself from others by my need to prove I was better than them. I wanted to be a leader. Instead, I was a complainer. The painful truth led me to learn how I could better work with others and, someday, lead them.

The best coaches make us recognize we have gaps in our reasoning. The moment we become unsure of what we know, learning happens. This is good coaching.

Even if all clients need from you in the moment is to be a sounding board as they sort through their thoughts, we can still use curiosity to *partner* with them to see themselves and the world in a broader way. Coaches facilitate this process in the way that Dewey imagined was possible.

WE'VE DRIFTED AWAY FROM THE INTENTION OF COACHING

My second master's degree is in adult learning/instructional design. I'll never forget a professor saying we should always tell students what they would be tested on so they could focus their learning. As a student, I loved this advice. My hope was to get an A in the class. I wasn't considering how I would apply what I learned when I graduated. I just wanted to learn enough to be an A student.

I still believe you should test what you teach, but a growing number of students in coach training programs worldwide are demanding to learn specific coaching steps to earn their credentials. The focus of learning has shifted to the test and away from the client relationship. ICF efforts to legitimize coaching by making it data-driven often overshadow the intention of coaching. Taking an evidence-based approach to limit assessor subjectivity is important, and behavioral descriptions are useful for trainers and mentors, but transferring specific requirements to students has contributed to thinking of coaching as a formulaic process. In attempts to make coaching memorable, the heart of coaching is disappearing.

The identified coaching competencies were never intended to be a checklist of behaviors. I was a part of the ICF leadership when the competencies were written. The focus was on the transformational experience where people learned from the inside out. The competencies weren't meant to be taken in any order other than the beginning and ending—to determine where the conversation is going and then to close it out with a commitment. The remaining competencies reflected how present coaches are with their clients. Coaches need to fully receive what their clients say and express with no judgment. Then they could competently be curious about intentions and meaning. There isn't one right way to coach; coaching is a spontaneous process between the coach and client.

> Coaching competencies provide the framework to facilitate self-discovery. They are not a checklist of required statements and questions.

The early ICF leaders committed to building the coaching profession because of the positive impact we believed coaching would make in the world. The emphasis was on establishing a safe and caring relationship between coach and client so people felt seen and valued. Then, once agreement was reached on the outcome they would attempt to achieve, the conversation flowed naturally from the coach's curiosity. The coach was not recalling memorized lists, models, and formulas. I am happy to see that the 2020 updated ICF competencies better reflect the aspirations of the founding members.

Coaching is more than reflecting and asking questions. Coaches must create a bond of trust that deepens over time. The relationship is essential for the coach to be an effective thinking partner. The courage, care, and curiosity coaches feel, and the belief they have in their clients' potential, make the competencies work.

During my first class at my coaching school, the founder, Thomas Leonard, said we can learn how to coach only by getting out there and coaching people. We resisted, saying we didn't know what to do. He said we would learn enough to start coaching after the first class, and then we should "just go love them."

I have used this advice for over twenty years. Most times, I feel my clients love me back.

I want to bring the heart as well as the art of coaching into all of our conversations about coaching. I wrote this book to be a guide for all people who use coaching, regardless of the school they attend, the credential they earn, and the role they play.

Although part II provides practices that will ensure coaching effectiveness, the mental habits in part III are essential for establishing the relationship that makes coaching so powerful. You won't find lists of what you should ask and say. You will discover how you can expand people's capacity to learn and grow together in our complex, uncertain world. I honor you for choosing this journey.

CHAPTER 1

WHAT MAKES COACHING THE PERSON SO POWERFUL?

Ideas are our rules—for better or worse.

—JOHN DEWEY

USING COACHING SKILLS has become a critical competency for leadership in global companies. Coaching credentials are required by most corporate buyers when hiring external coaches, even when they aren't sure what the credentials represent.

On the consumer side, awareness of the value of coaching is growing.[1] Unfortunately, according to the Federal Trade Commission, some people still lose a great deal of money to those who sell "business coaching packages" that promise big money from their programs.[2] Though the number of individuals hiring coaches is growing worldwide, we still have work to do to teach the public how to evaluate if coaches and programs adhere to professional standards so the value of professional coaching continues to grow.

The success and ongoing growth of coaching is due to one fact: it works. Other attempts at motivation and influence aren't as effective.

HOW COACHING WORKS

Most people don't relate coaching to the important work of John Dewey. They will tell you coaching came from the first founders of coaching schools, the teachings of Sir John Whitmore or Carl Rogers, neurolinguistic programming masters, or their favorite leadership book. These are great sources of coaching tools. The reason these tools work could be found in John Dewey's writing long before our current coaching gurus were born.

Coaching is valuable because none of us transform our thinking on our own. Humans are masters at rationalizing hastily made choices no matter how logical we think we are. We're also exceptional at blaming whomever or whatever we can when those choices turn out badly.

As Daniel Kahneman said in his book *Thinking, Fast and Slow*, we resist self-exploration especially when emotions are involved. We don't change well on our own. To stop adverse thinking patterns, someone outside our head needs to disrupt our thinking by reflecting our thoughts back to us and asking questions that prompt us to wonder why we think the way we do.[3] These statements and questions enable us to see our concocted stories as if they were laid out in front of us in a book to be read and analyzed.

Adults need this help to expand their thinking as much as children do, and sometimes more. As we age, we become more rigid in our thinking. We become masters at rationalizing our actions, ignoring our emotions, and finding what confirms our beliefs. We don't distance ourselves from social pressures. We're too busy to stop and examine our beliefs and choices.

Dewey said that reflective inquiry would not only open a person to learning but also bring to light stereotypes and inherited biases. By bringing beliefs, assumptions, fears, needs, and conflicts of values to the surface, a person can better evaluate decisions and actions. He also said provoking people to think about their thinking was the "single most powerful antidote to erroneous beliefs and autopilot."[4]

When we are willing, reflective practices lead us to say, "Wow, look at what I'm doing to myself." Sometimes we say, "Those aren't my words. Someone gave them to me." We become objective observers of our stories.

Reflections followed by questions prompt us to stop and question our thinking and behaviors. This disruption initiates a shift in how we see ourselves and the world, or at least how we are framing a dilemma. We see a new way forward with a stronger commitment to taking action than if we were told what we should do by an expert.

> Reflective statements help people think about what they are saying. The follow-up question seals the deal, creating the shift in awareness that resolves issues and prompts new actions.

Dewey also said the most intelligent people need the most help thinking about their thinking. Smart people are the best rationalizers. They believe their reasoning wholeheartedly and will protect their opinions as solid facts. Telling them to change is a waste of time. Using strong reflections and questions is the only way to get smart people to question their thoughts.

Leadership expert Hal Gregersen says unexpected shifts are always around the corner in life and business.[5] We must go beyond the bounds of what we know. Because our brains resist this exploration when left to their own devices, we can navigate daily dilemmas better with coaches who use reflective inquiry.

YOUR BRAIN ON COACHING

To go about our days without having to think through every action, our brains develop constructs and rules we operate with unconsciously. Neuroscientist Michael Gazzaniga says we get stuck in our automatic thought processing and fool ourselves into thinking we are acting consciously and willfully.[6]

> For the same reason you can't tickle yourself, your brain resists self-imposed testing of thoughts and reactions.

Then, to protect our identity and routines, when someone questions our choices without asking permission, we quickly defend ourselves. We angrily respond when our beliefs are challenged. Unless we invite the assessment, we fortify our defensive walls to protect our perspective. Even if an argument makes sense, we're more likely to find a reason for our beliefs than recognize the flaws.

To think differently, we need to invite someone to help us examine our thinking. Only then do we dare stop the brain from quickly reacting. Disruption must be welcomed to interrupt our automatic thought processing.

Enter the coach. If we seek coaching, we are inviting the external interruption that compels us to stop and examine our thinking and behavior. Our brains resist a surprise attack from someone who points out faults in our thinking. Knowing the value of coaching, we willingly invite a coach to look for these faults together with us.

Coaching versus Telling

Many leaders think it is easier to give advice than to take the time to coach others to find their own solutions. They don't realize they are wasting time instead of saving it.

When you tell people what to do, you tap into their cognitive brain, where they can analyze your words using what they already know. If what you suggest relates to or affirms their current knowledge, they are likely to agree with you. They might have needed outside confirmation to fortify their confidence before acting.

Offering ideas might sound like an efficient way to guide people's actions. This is true, but you also run the risk of making them dependent on you for answers or approval before they act. You won't create independent thinkers.

The results are even less productive if they didn't seek your counsel. They might hear you but then forget what you said in a very short time. The cognitive brain uses short-term memory, which is limited by both time and capacity. Other issues rank higher in importance, edging out your requests and ideas. We often don't remember what we ate for breakfast much less what someone told us to do.

Even if you do remember what someone told you during the day, you will lose the memory once you go to sleep. The brain sorts through input from the day to determine what is worth saving in long-term memory. It retains bits of information that triggered emotions; emotions tell the brain that something is important to remember. Unless you inspire people with your ideas or shock them with a unique perspective, they won't remember what you said the next day. Or they might remember but confuse details when they attempt to reconstruct what you said. We alter our memories every time we recall them.

Remember all those quizzes you took in grade school to test your learning? How many would you pass today? Unless you continually use the information you memorized, it is lost. The brain finds no reason for keeping it.

> When we tell people what to do, we access their short-term memory in their cognitive brain, where learning is least effective.

The cognitive brain may be good at problem-solving, but it's not so good at learning. Also, if people come to depend on you for answers, they lose motivation to think for themselves. This approach may work for consultants who want long-term work, but it's not the best when you are a leader, parent, teacher, or coach who wants to help people think for themselves.

Coaching versus Threatening: The Feedback Myth

When people experience a threat, they move into a defensive position. Threats include negative feedback and what people must do "or else." If they comply, their brains lodge the direction given along with the feedback as critical to implement. Fear-based learning is encoded as a survival response in the primitive brain. When faced with similar situations, people react in a way to avoid the threat of "or else" and receive the reward for behaving correctly, even if circumstances have changed. Their brains don't trust being told to act differently. Resistance to change occurs because the current behavior was learned through fear.

> Learning based in fear fortifies behavior. The brain then resists change. Survival-based learning limits risk taking and agility.

Additionally, giving feedback often triggers stress, shame, and fear. The helpful information you give people often raises defenses or lowers confidence, decreasing initiative and innovation.

In the article "Find the Coaching in Criticism," Harvard Law professors Sheila Heen and Douglas Stone found that even well-intentioned opinions "spark an emotional reaction, inject tension into the relationship, and bring communication to a halt" no matter the position or years of experience of either the leader or feedback recipient. People want to learn and grow, but they also have a basic human need for acceptance. Feedback, especially if unsolicited, is painful.[7]

The leaders I coach still tell me that people want feedback. Yet their direct reports tell me when I interview them that they want to improve but don't want more feedback. They want two-way conversations that pull out their ideas and open their eyes to greater possibilities, not one-way directives focused on what they did wrong.

Unfortunately, coaching is often confused with giving feedback. Even if feedback is received well, if you then tell people what to do instead, you aren't coaching them to determine what they can do differently to get better results.

Unless someone asks for your advice because they truly don't have a clue what to do, your feedback creates resistance or compliance. You stunt instead of grow people's minds.

Coaching Taps into the Middle Brain

When it comes to influencing a change in behavior, you want to activate people's creative minds instead of their survival or analytical mechanisms. You don't start by telling them what they did wrong. When you ask people to review what happened in a situation, they usually know what didn't work. People tend to be their harshest critics. Ask them to assess their behavior first. They might then ask for help on how to change. Even then, you want to explore their ideas before offering your own.

The middle brain houses long-term memory. Tapping into people's prior knowledge to strategize a new way forward arouses both a positive sense of responsibility and courage. If improvement conversations started with a coaching approach instead of feedback, they would activate creativity instead of provoking defensiveness.

A reflective inquiry–based conversation focused on how people think facilitates insight-based learning. Creative thoughts emerge as people pull out and connect bits of stored information in a new way to answer a provocative question. When their thoughts, beliefs, and emotional reactions are held up in reflection, they are prompted to examine their thinking. As their reasoning and justifications begin to unravel, their brain quickly reorders bits of information to make more sense. They have an insight that feels like an *aha moment*. Their perception changes. They gain a new awareness of themselves and the world around them. Insight-based learning develops people's minds and confidence.

Using reflective statements and questions in a way that prompts people to examine what they are thinking incites creative breakthroughs. You are cracking the ego walls that protect how they see themselves and what they believe should happen in the world around them. For a moment, they will stare at you as their brains go offline to make sense of what is being altered in their stories and definitions. The first glimpse at this new truth could cause an emotional reaction before the insight is clear enough for them to articulate. If you help them solidify the new awareness by asking what they are now seeing or learning, you fortify the shift.[8]

Consider a time you felt stuck sorting out a work relationship that had soured. The sudden, new solution to the problem probably didn't come to you as you hovered over your desk ruminating over past conversations. The insight that showed you a new way to approach the situation likely came as a result of a statement made or question posed by someone else.

When someone you trust challenges your reasoning and asks you a question that breaks through your protective frame, your brain is forced to reorder data in your long-term memory. For a moment, the breakdown feels awkward. In the midst of this discomfort, your brain is most open to learning. A new, broader perspective forms. You may feel a range of emotions from sad to outright angry for not seeing the truth before. You might feel vulnerable, embarrassed, and even scared. Often, my clients laugh at what they see—after they gasp.

Coaching that uses a reflective inquiry approach improves both outcomes and satisfaction. People want two-way conversations that pull out their ideas and open their eyes to greater possibilities, not one-way directives focused on what they did wrong.

Sometimes, a course correction is vital. But if the smart people you are coaching know what to do but aren't doing it, the conversation should focus on what is stopping them from applying what they know, not on giving feedback and advice.

Case Study

I had a client who disrespected her peers in strategy meetings. Her leader could not get through to her with feedback, even though she wanted the promotion he wouldn't give her until she earned the respect of her peers. She had made some behavioral shifts. She quit openly criticizing her peers in meetings. Instead, when their ideas ran counter to hers, she rolled her eyes and sighed. Exasperated, her manager asked me to coach her.

After determining she was willing to be coached, we explored what annoyed her about her peers' ideas. At one point, she said with a sarcastic tone, "Their ideas are typical to Latinos." I reflected the judgment I heard in her belief and asked what made their perspective wrong. This led to a discussion about different views of leadership based on culture. My client was from Germany and had lived in Central America for two years. Finally, my client blurted, "Leaders should make efficiency their priority." I asked what her peers thought should be the leader's priority. She conceded they would choose employee engagement, where people enjoyed working together.

As we unwrapped the beliefs and values she held in contrast to her peers, my client said she knew she couldn't bully them to accept her views. Maybe they could compromise. If she could involve them in a conversation, she might find a way to integrate their priorities. We then explored what she could do differently to mitigate the negative judgment her peers had of her so they might be open to brainstorm with her. She also realized she needed to re-earn their trust. She chose to set up one-on-one meetings with her peers to repair the relationships. They would meet over lunch since she knew they liked to share meals. She would genuinely ask what they thought she could do to be a better team member.

Feedback pushed her to *pretend* to behave differently. Coaching shifted her perspective, which allowed her to discover how to achieve her goals on her own. The way she reframed how values defined leadership, as well as what were essential versus adaptive practices, changed her behavior for good.

WHEN TO COACH AND WHEN NOT TO

Many coaches will tell you they do "hybrid coaching" that blends mentoring into the conversation. They say people want our opinions and the benefits of our experiences. They explore their clients' views of a problem and then tell them what to do.

> There is no such thing as hybrid coaching.

You are either coaching or you're doing something else. Something else might be exactly what someone needs, but this is not true in every situation.

Some well-known coaches declare just asking questions wastes people's time. They staunchly defend their reasons for giving advice.

I agree—only asking questions is a waste of time. Coaching includes reflective practices, such as summarizing, noticing emotional shifts, and acknowledging courageous actions. Reflections can be just as powerful as or more powerful than solo questions.

The notion of hybrid coaching dilutes the value of coaching. When you mix mentoring, advice giving, and leading people to what is best for them into what you call coaching, people come to expect the easy way out. They look forward to your telling them what to do. This might be helpful, but if coaching is what they really want or need, they miss experiencing this powerful technology for creating breakthroughs and growth.

Many times, people don't want or need coaching.

You need to determine with them what they want from you. Then call what you are doing what it is—coaching or something else.

First Establish a Desire for Coaching

Once, when a colleague tried to coach me on a situation when I only wanted to talk, I shut her down. "Stop coaching me. Right now, I just need a friend." That incident made me look at the times when I butted in, trying to coach my friends.

Outside a formally declared coaching session, ask people if they would like some coaching before you start probing. You might ask, "What do you need from me right now?" They might just want to be listened to, especially if they are outraged about a situation or they are grieving a loss.

Even if they say they want coaching, make sure they are willing to engage with you. They must demonstrate a willingness to question their own thoughts and motivations, not just seek affirmation for their views. For example, they might want you to hear them create a plan, but they aren't open to being coached around the plan's purpose, practicality, or contingencies.

Some people are verbal processors, meaning they think best out loud with someone present. If they say they just want to think through a situation or sort out options, ask, "What kind of sounding board would be most useful?" A little bit of reflection—summarizing and paraphrasing—might be welcome. Ask before you interrupt their flow.

> No matter how masterful of a coach you are, someone must demonstrate a willingness to engage in coaching for you to be effective.

However, don't assume defensiveness means they are uncoachable. Ask what is causing the pushback or uncertainty. They may be wary but willing to explore what else could work.

Next, Be Sure Coaching Is the Right Option

Sometimes people lack experience and knowledge to draw on to formulate a new perspective. You can't coach something out of nothing.

Be careful—this deficit is real. When people say they have no idea what to do, ask if they have no idea or if they are questioning a solution that comes to mind. I often find that people who say they don't know what to do actually do know. They have a solution but are afraid to use it. In such cases, I might say, "You have many life experiences. I bet you have some ideas" or "If you had nothing to lose, what would you try?" or "Have you ever observed someone else in this position or scenario—might you try what you observed or do the opposite?" If they still have no ideas, put on your mentoring hat and offer options.

Coaching is best used when clients have some knowledge and skills to draw on but they aren't sure about the options, what's best to do first, or the reasons for their own uncertainty. If they have a decision to make but are confused by the shoulds that bombard their brains or they are afraid of making a wrong move, they will benefit from coaching.

You can always start with coaching. If you discover they don't have the experience or knowledge to know what to do, you can ask if you can step out of coaching to offer suggestions.

Remember, the key word that differentiates what coaches do is *partnering*. Coaches are *thinking partners*. We do not see our clients as clueless or needing to be fixed. They often can use their creativity and resources to solve their own problems through a coaching conversation that focuses on seeing beyond their blocks.

When I teach coaching skills, I ask my students, "Are you willing to give up being the one who knows best to be the coach?" You must step out of being the expert, fixer, or helper to coach.

Learn When Not to Coach

Do not coach if you can't do the following:

+ *Let go of how you want the conversation to go.* You want clients to resolve their problems, but you can't be attached to how the conversation will progress or what the outcome will be. If you can't detach, you will end up forcing the conversation in the direction you want it to go.

+ *Believe in the clients' ability to figure out what to do.* Do you have any judgments about your clients that could get in the way? If you doubt their ability to find a way forward, then choose to mentor instead. Otherwise, your impatience will impact your conversations even if you have been trained to put on a poker face.

+ *Feel hopeful, curious, and care.* If you are angry or disappointed with clients, they will react to your emotions more than your words. If you are afraid the conversations won't go well, do what you can to release your fear so you model what courage and optimism feel like.

Not all conversations can or should be coaching sessions. Figure out what people need and then choose to coach or do something else.

IDEAL COACHING SCENARIOS

Opportunities to coach people often show up in these scenarios, including both personal and work circumstances:

+ Exploring ways to improve communications
+ Facing fears of conflict and emotional reactions in oneself and others
+ Finding solutions for dealing with difficult people and situations
+ Strengthening relationships at work and home
+ Articulating desires and visions, both personally and professionally
+ Managing stress and well-being to maximize energy
+ Sorting through difficult decisions
+ Experiencing greater fulfillment and success
+ Dealing with work and life changes
+ Leading through changes in the organization and in the world
+ Inspiring greater team performance
+ Aligning leadership teams
+ Shifting the corporate culture
+ Increasing employee engagement throughout the organization
+ Identifying development paths, both preparing for and succeeding in new roles

At work, you can also use coaching to better connect and engage with others. A survey published in *Harvard Business Review* found young high achievers were often dissatisfied with the lack of mentoring and coaching they received.[9] A good way of engaging people is to be curious about what they want for their futures or ask what they need right now to overcome challenges and then listen to their responses. They want conversations that expand their minds as well as their skills.

For coaching to be successful, clients should know what will occur in a typical coaching session. Conversations about the coaching process generally happen at the beginning of a coaching relationship. Clients should also be told they will experience the best outcomes if they do the following:

- Respond to reflective statements and questions, even when it feels uncomfortable. This is the best opportunity for a breakthrough!
- Be an active participant, not a curious bystander.
- Be open, honest, and willing to explore what isn't clear or fully known about themselves, others, and the situation.
- Meet commitments for action between sessions and show up for scheduled sessions unless an unexpected emergency emerges.
- Carve out time to think about the coaching conversation after a session and immediately before the next session.

Coaching has found its place in our world. It is a valuable way to facilitate behavioral change. Coaching helps people think more broadly for themselves when they feel challenged or unsure and provides clarity and direction for people who want to accomplish more.

CHAPTER 2

CRAZY COACHING BELIEFS

If you are following a formula or model,
you aren't really coaching.

—MARCIA REYNOLDS

SOME COACHES, COACHING schools, and credentialing organizations don't follow the ICF coaching competencies and get amazing results. No matter what theoretical framework they draw from, if they predominantly use reflective inquiry, I support their approaches. The essence of coaching is congruent with the practices taught in this book no matter their philosophy and implementation.

There isn't one right way to coach. If your practice encourages your clients to self-reflect and generate insight, we are speaking the same language. If you don't know all the answers and are comfortable with not knowing, we can disagree on competencies while agreeing on the power of coaching.

Conversely, certain beliefs and judgments about coaching belittle our work and hurt our profession. Some assumptions steer leaders away from using a coaching approach in their conversations. Some coaches plateau in their development when they adhere to rigid rules about how they ask questions or think they have to use a model with specific steps to coach well.

> The unreasonable beliefs, judgments, and assumptions about coaching have increased over the years as coaching has grown in popularity.

At least five crazy coaching beliefs have thrown the value of coaching offtrack. I will explain each one, why all of them may be true sometimes, and how they limit the effectiveness of coaching when interpreted as rigid rules. I will also offer an alternative opinion for each belief and show how it works within the framework of the coaching relationship.

CRAZY BELIEF #1: IT TAKES A LONG TIME TO BE REALLY GOOD AT COACHING

Where the Belief Comes From

New coaches love seeing demonstrations by experienced coaches. Even if the experienced coach breaks down how the coaching was done after the session—what clues she picked up; what contradictions, emotional shifts, and repeated words she noticed; and what beliefs stood out as significant to confront—the observers declare the session a magic act.

Observing a performance by someone who has thousands of hours of practice conjures both awe and doubt—awe for the mastery and doubt by less experienced coaches that they can ever achieve the feat themselves. This is especially true when the person demonstrating the coaching doesn't consider the developmental level of the audience. The demonstration shows off the coach's skills more than providing a learning experience. Observers are scared into thinking they can't actively coach until they are "good enough."

In addition to observing demonstrations, coaches working to earn their credentials must receive mentoring. Mentoring, whether with a group or one-on-one, includes feedback. As described in the previous chapter, feedback induces stress and can decrease confidence. The mentoring is meant to help—it usually does—yet the process can add to the belief that coaching takes a long time to learn.

What Is True about the Belief

Undoing habits of thinking takes time. Both new and experienced coaches want to feel helpful and useful, which is why they jump to finding solutions before exploring context and blocks. Undoing the tendency to leap to options takes deliberate practice and patience. Being comfortable with just being curious requires the willingness to feel uncomfortable with not knowing the answers.

There is a reason that it takes hundreds of coaching hours to earn a credential. So far, no one has invented a magic pill that lets people instantly master coaching ability. Practice is necessary. To achieve levels of mastery, there is no substitute for consistently coaching and hiring coaching mentors to help you progress.

Every year since I started, I become a better coach. I may have been a good coach years ago, but good coaching gets better as I continue to coach, teach, and mentor. Mastery is a journey with no ending.

What Is Not True and Limiting

Don't listen when your brain tells you *you shouldn't coach until you finish your coach training and feel confident about your skills.*

When I started teaching coaching skills a few years into my business, I painfully saw the gaps in my coaching as I taught others how to coach. Yet even in my first few years of coaching imperfectly, my client testimonials were glowing. My clients felt safe enough with me to talk things through. They felt stronger about their choices and plans. They saw their context and blocks more clearly through my limited use of coaching.

You do not have to wait before you coach. Even new coaches provide a great service if the conversation feels safe and judgment free. Don't wait until you feel confident enough to coach people outside your family or coaching peers. Every adult can benefit from a thinking partner.

Alternative Opinion

There is no perfect coach. You start, and then with practice, good mentoring, and continuous learning, you discover the power of coaching well. You have to coach to improve your skills.

I believe all people who want to coach well should get solid coach training, preferably from an accredited school or recognized academic program. Just because your family and friends say you should be a coach doesn't mean you were born with the skills. You might be a good, empathic listener. This is a great foundation to build on. Learning the five essential practices in this book will help, but the skills are best learned from qualified coach trainers.

Once you learn the basics, go coach. If you resist giving advice, you won't cause harm. As my mentor used to say, "No one ever died from coaching."

What makes coaching so powerful is the relationship between the coach and client. That is why this book provides three mental habits to make your five essential practices effective. If clients feel safe with you, you create the circumstances for learning to happen even when your skills aren't developed. If you believe in their ability to think through their dilemmas; if you learn how to catch and release your judgments and fears; and then you stay patient, curious, and sincerely care about them, they will find value in coaching.

CRAZY BELIEF #2: QUESTIONS ARE NEEDED TO CREATE A BREAKTHROUGH OR NEW AWARENESS

Where the Belief Comes From

Although the use of reflective statements is taught by many coaching schools, questions still win the popularity contest. Some schools teach that coaching is only a series of open-ended questions. Popular books tout the best questions for leaders and coaches to use. When a coach demonstrates coaching, observers often highlight the best questions asked. They don't recall the reflective statements that prompted self-reflection. The powerful question gets the glory.

What Is True about the Belief

A good question can disturb people's equilibrium enough to test the validity or absurdity of their thoughts and beliefs. Instead of thinking about a problem, they examine the thinking that made the issue a problem. Instead of quickly considering options and actions, they stop and reflect on their beliefs and perceptions, which can change their view on what actions to take.

Every action we take has a reason. We don't recognize the faults in our reasoning unless someone questions our thinking. Questions help us assess our beliefs and perceptions against the context and possibilities in a way we can't do for ourselves.

What Is Not True and Limiting

Don't believe people who say *coaching and asking questions are synonymous.*

Coaching is a process of inquiry, not a series of questions. The intent of inquiry is to provoke critical thinking to discern gaps in logic, evaluate the value of beliefs, and clarify fears, doubts, and desires affecting our outlook and behavior.

Some people think sticking to questions keeps coaches from slanting the conversation with their opinions and biases. Yet even questions can be tainted by opinions and biases, leading the client to the coach's way of thinking. Plus the time it takes to conjure up a good stand-alone question takes away from one's coaching presence.

Coaching as a series of questions can feel like an interrogation, damaging trust and rapport. Without reflective statements, questions feel more like an impersonal formula than a spontaneous process.

Alternative Opinion

The opposite of giving advice is not asking questions. The use of *reflective statements,* such as summarizing, encapsulating, and sharing observed emotional shifts as described in the following chapters, can be more powerful than seeking the magical question. Hearing someone restate your words can be shocking, especially if you have been saying the same words for years. Having someone share the emotions you attach to different ideas and hold out the contradictions in your statements for you to witness can break down defenses of ancient beliefs more effectively than a provocative question.

Adding reflective statements to questions makes coaching feel more natural and effortless. When the coach first reflects words and expressions and then asks a question, the question is more likely to arise out of curiosity, not memory.

When you are racking your brain to remember a good question, you are in your head and not present. You miss when clients tell you what they really want or when they reveal the belief or fear that is paralyzing. Being present is more important than being perfect.

CRAZY BELIEF #3: THE COACH MUST ASK ONLY OPEN, NOT CLOSED, QUESTIONS

Where the Belief Comes From

Closed questions tend to generate one-word yes or no answers. Whether learning coaching, counseling, law, journalism, or any other practice where you need a person to provide information, the texts tout the use of open-ended questions to get full answers. Some coaching schools prohibit the use of closed questions. People who assess the recordings of coaching sessions to determine if the coach performed well enough to earn an ICF credential will count the number of open and closed questions to ensure more open questions are used. Many coaches declare closed questions are the antithesis of good coaching and negatively judge an experienced coach who uses them.

What Is True about the Belief

One-word answers to questions shut down instead of open up a conversation. These moments can make the coach uncomfortable, feeling there is nowhere to go in the conversation. The coach may even repeat the closed question to verify the answer while desperately thinking about what to say next.

The use of closed questions with clients at the beginning of a coaching relationship can be deadly. If clients don't trust the coach, closed questions allow them to maintain their defenses. They won't look into their thoughts. They deflect attempts to explore their beliefs. They won't reveal the emotions they feel other than irritation with the coach.

Closed questions can also be leading statements in disguise. When coaches think they know what clients should do, they will use a closed question to force a perspective. Examples of suggestions disguised as questions start with "Have you tried . . ." or "What if you were to . . ." The coach might offer a good idea but deter clients from thinking through situations themselves. Clients might take the suggestion to please the coach.

Open questions that start with *what, where, when, how,* and *who* will get more than one-word responses. Open, exploratory questions incite a deeper look at what is prompting behavior or inaction. Even reluctant clients might recognize the limits of their perspective when asked open questions.

What Is Not True and Limiting

Don't believe people when they say *closed questions get closed answers in all situations; they are used only by inexperienced coaches.*

A client had left her job to recover from burnout. She enjoyed fixing up her house, playing with her child, and traveling with friends for six months. Then the restlessness kicked in. She asked her coach to help her decide what she should do next. The coach asked her questions about what she most missed about her last job and the parts she hoped she would never have to do again.

The coach summarized, "You love creating new things with a team of competent people. You don't care for development conversations with lower level employees. Is this true?" She answered, "Exactly," and went on to further describe what she loved most about her last position. The coach then asked, "Does this reflection give you any idea about what you want to create now?" The client said, "Yes," and went on to describe what an ideal job would look like. The coach then said, "You clearly miss working with a team on exciting new projects. You could do this freelancing, but you kept putting yourself inside an organization when you described your ideal situation. Have you already decided to focus on landing a new job as your next step?" The client sighed, agreed, and explained her fears. Three closed questions led to further exploration.

When the coach has a strong relationship with the client, closed questions can be just as provocative as open questions. The purpose of questions is to disrupt a pattern or flow of thinking and prompt deeper exploration. The focus of a question should be on whether it opens or closes the client's mind. As long as the question furthers the conversation, it shouldn't matter how it is structured.

Alternative Opinion

Closed questions are effective in at least three situations: (1) to help clarify what clients want to resolve in the coaching, (2) to affirm if a reflective statement is accurate, and (3) to prompt clients when it is clear they have had a startling insight but they aren't speaking. In the last case, a question such as "Has something shifted for you?" might give them the push they need to articulate what they now see.

One of the five essential practices—goaltending—is to unwrap and clarify the desired outcome. After hearing the client's story, the coach needs to know what is important for the client to achieve in the session. The coach might use closed questions to affirm the direction of the conversation. Then, while telling his story, the client might reveal two or more outcomes he would like to manifest. The coach summarizes the options presented and then invites the client to choose one outcome to work on first. While exploring what needs to be achieved, resolved, or understood for the client to move forward, a new more important outcome might show up, such as building confidence, changing a habit, or accepting an uncomfortable reality. The coach then asks if the client wants to shift the outcome based on what was revealed. These closed questions offer clarity and confirmation.

Closed questions can be used to test the validity of a reflective statement. For example, when you summarize what is heard and expressed, notice shifts in emotions, or identify underlying beliefs or assumptions, you might ask if the client agrees with the summary, observation, or inference. Even in these situations, the client tends to provide more information, not a one-word answer.

When clients trust you are there to help them achieve something important to them, they will accept the discomfort of an edgy closed question. For example, if they realize their actions have been sabotaging their desires, you might ask, "Will you ever be content with the situation as it is?" or "Are you willing to look at what you might change to get what you really want?" or "Will you regret not taking action a year from now?" You might follow up these closed questions with an open question about what they want to look at or do next, but the closed question provides the push off the fence.

For closed questions to be effective, clients must know you believe they are smart and resourceful. They must know you are not trying to make them feel wrong or inadequate. Closed questions that follow summaries, such as, "Is this correct?" or "Do you want to change this pattern?" or "Do you know if your expectation is realistic?" can help crystalize thoughts if asked with sincere interest.

Quit condemning closed questions. They are good clarifiers and can provoke examination. Let's bring them back into our training so coaches know how to use them well.

CRAZY BELIEF #4:
REFLECTIVE STATEMENTS ARE TOO CONFRONTATIONAL

Where the Belief Comes From

Coaches are often relieved when they hear me use reflective statements, especially in the Americas and Europe. They say, "You can do that? That makes coaching so much easier!" They thought reflective statements, like closed questions, were wrong to use because they would lead the client to a specific answer.

The reaction to my frequent use of reflective statements is more profound in the Middle East and Asia. People in these regions equate reflective statements with direct communications. In their cultures, being direct with someone is confrontational and harmful. When I mentor these coaches, they tell me I don't understand their cultures—it's impolite to be so direct.

What Is True about the Belief

The emotions felt when delivering a reflective statement impact the reaction. If you don't offer your statements with curiosity and care, clients may feel you are being confrontational.

If your intention is to show clients the fault in their thinking, they will feel manipulated. They will shut down.

When you feel impatient or uncomfortable, your reflective statements feel judgmental or pushy. Clients might feel you are criticizing them. They may retreat with irritation. Or they may become compliant, looking for you to tell them what to think and do differently.

What Is Not True and Limiting

Don't accept the belief that *reflective statements will lead the client in a specific direction; they are confrontational.*

Feedback often feels hurtful. Abruptly responding to clients with advice or a judgmental view of their ideas will distance you from your clients, regardless of geographic location. Giving feedback and judging client responses are not the same as using the reflective statements taught in this book.

Alternative Opinion

If you actively replay the client's expressed words and emotions *with no attachment to being right or to provoking a specific response,* you are not being overly directive. Reflective statements feel confrontational only when the coach is impatient or unsettled.

A reflective statement may challenge the substance of your clients' beliefs, perplexing the brain in a way that feels uncomfortable, embarrassing, or confusing. If you remain calm, holding a quiet, safe space for clients to work through their emotions, the reaction fades. If you then ask them what they now understand, you help them articulate a more constructive perception that helps them find a way to move toward their desired outcome. Even if they are uncomfortable as they recognize how their thoughts and behaviors are limiting them, they feel more confident at the end of the coaching session.

CRAZY BELIEF #5: COACHING MUST ALWAYS HAVE A CLEAR OUTCOME OR VISION OF A DESIRED FUTURE

Where the Belief Comes From

I am not aware of any coach training that doesn't include how to establish a desired outcome or goal of the coaching session. The Coaching Research Laboratory at the Weatherhead School of Management, Case Western Reserve University, touts the power of positive visioning in the coaching process.[1] When you have an end in mind, instead of focusing on a problem to be solved, the coaching moves toward a picture of what is possible. Focusing on a desired future keeps the conversation appreciative, making it inspiring, strength based, and self-directed.

What Is True about the Belief

One of the most important yet difficult aspects of coaching is to keep the conversation on track to a fulfilling resolution. Although the direction of coaching can change many times in one conversation, the final destination needs to be clarified for any sense of forward movement to be felt.

When the desired outcome of the coaching session stays vague, the conversation goes in circles. Clients might declare next steps, but they probably won't implement them. They might have enjoyed talking about their problem in a safe space, but nothing was resolved.

What Is Not True and Limiting

It is not always true that *the client must have a clear vision of a desired future at the start of the coaching conversation.*

Clients are often unsure what they want from coaching at the outset. The best they can do is describe the decision that has them perplexed or the clarity they need about a situation.

Once, in a group mentoring session, the coach was urging the client to create a clear, positive picture of the future she wanted to create. The client said she wasn't ready to do that. She wanted to talk about the options she had at the moment before she could determine which future she wanted to envision. The coach kept urging her to share what her best future looked like. The client defiantly resisted. The coach asked her to stand up and walk toward her future to see what might become clear. The client pursed her lips and started crying. I stopped the session before more damage was done.

The coach had been trained to create a clear, positive vision at the start of coaching. This made her performance formulaic. She no longer was present to her client's needs. It's not that a desired future wasn't possible to imagine, it just wasn't possible at that time.

Alternative Opinion

The outcome of a coaching conversation must be clear, but it often evolves as the coaching progresses. At the beginning of a session, clients might only be able to state a desire for clarity around what is making them feel stuck or unsure. As the session progresses, the fear, need, or conflict of values that is paralyzing their brains may emerge. From here, a new outcome may come to light. This new outcome will probably be more personal, such as "developing the confidence needed to take more risks." The coaching shifts in this new direction. This shift can happen a few times in a session as clients sort deeper through their thoughts and emotions, revealing what they *really* want to happen and what is *really* getting in the way.

Also, success in a session may not always include steps toward a tangible outcome. You must meet your clients at the point where they are willing to go. Processing new information can take days. You should still get a commitment from clients on when and how they will take time to think about what occurred in the coaching. If they meet their commitment, they may make a decision or take significant steps before the next session.

Sometimes the best learning happens in the time between coaching sessions.

PART II

THE FIVE ESSENTIAL PRACTICES

*When we question what we know, we are
open to learning. We just don't do this well
when left to figure things out on our own.*

—MARCIA REYNOLDS

MANY COACHING MODELS can lead to a satisfying outcome for the client. Just creating a safe space for people to pause and sort through their thoughts can be beneficial. Coaching models provide value if three goals are met: (1) an outcome for the coaching session is identified, even if it evolves; (2) blocks, or what needs to be resolved by the client, are discovered; and (3) an achievable next step is articulated.

These three goals of all effective coaching models provide focus and movement in the coaching conversation. The outcome defines what the person wants to get as a result of the conversation. The blocks are the emotions, beliefs, or conflicts that are deterring the client from achieving the outcome. Specifying and committing to take at least one step forward ensures progress between sessions even if the next step is "I need to take time to think about it."

Identifying an outcome, sorting through options and consequences, and then making a plan can be used for basic problem-solving. We call this *coaching at a surface level*, or *transactional coaching*. These types of conversations are beneficial, especially when clients are verbal processors—people who need to think out loud—and they feel safe talking with you. I sometimes have these conversations with my clients but not all the time. Being a sounding board in every session is not worth their money or my time. The coaching stays focused on the problem, not the people who see the situation as a problem.

What is more useful is to utilize my coach training and experience to look at what is making this situation a problem they can't sort out on their own. How is their thinking contributing to the dilemmas they are facing? The second step in the coaching models differentiates coaching from problem-solving. The methods used to discover what needs to be resolved by the client are key to transforming thinking. We coach people to see the problem and possibilities in new ways. Clients gain a broader view of themselves and their circumstances, changing how they handle their interactions and decisions going forward.

TRANSACTIONAL VERSUS TRANSFORMATIONAL COACHING

Transactional coaching occurs when you assist clients to explore their thoughts about a situation so they can decide what to do, or not do, next. The conversation tends to follow a logical progression. You use a lot of "if . . . , then," "for what reasons," and "what else is possible" prompts for analysis. Clients may look backward to discern factors that led to the present moment. You may guide them to look forward to what might happen next and after that and after that. You might even explore the present moment to help clients separate what is feasible from what is a pipe dream.

No matter what direction you take, transactional coaching is linear and externally focused on the problem. Such conversations skim the surface instead of delving into the clients' thought patterns, biases, and emotional filters. Clients might thank you and commit to an action plan. However, once they face their daily dilemmas, the plan is often altered or forgotten.

Not every conversation needs to explore beliefs and blocks, but even a little dip in the pool to test an assumption or recognize an avoidance is useful. When people live with beliefs and behaviors for a long time, a transactional, problem-solving approach to change is not effective. Neuroscientist Michael Gazzaniga says we spend our days in automatic thought processing, rarely stopping to question the reasoning for our choices. Even when we do, our brains resist self-analysis to keep us feeling safe and right, even if we have a sense that our excuses are irrational. Someone outside our brains is needed to break through these protective devices with a transformational approach.[1]

Transformational coaching works from the inside out. Reflective inquiry is a powerful way to create the disruptions in thinking that lead to breakthrough transformation and change. This is when coaching feels magical.

Using reflective inquiry, clients see their beliefs as if they were laid out on a table to examine. From this vantage point, they can see the holes in their logic or an outdated point of view. Further reflections and questions may reveal unspoken fears, needs, and desires. How clients frame reality morphs as they form new perceptions and beliefs.

> When clients attach new meaning to themselves and the world around them, their capabilities, their limitations, and what they define as right and wrong shift. The shifts cause changes in their choices and behavior.

Coaching the person, not the problem, by using reflective inquiry is the cornerstone of transformational coaching. The five essential practices described in the next five chapters will give you the reflective inquiry tools you need. Using these tools will improve your coaching no matter what school you attend and model you use. The reflective inquiry toolbox includes the following:

1. Focus—coaching the person, not the problem
2. Active Replay—playing back the pivotal pieces for review
3. Brain Hacking—finding the treasures in the box
4. Goaltending—staying the course
5. New and Next—coaxing insights and commitments

CHAPTER 3

FOCUS

Coaching the Person, Not the Problem

The client always knows more than
you do about what to do next.

—MARCIA REYNOLDS

MOST PROBLEM-SOLVING FORMULAS, and even some coaching models, focus on finding a solution to a problem. Coaching sessions generally start with clients describing a dilemma they are facing or naming a topic they want to discuss. It's a good place to start. However, once clients share their stories and define what they believe to be the problem, it's the wrong place to focus the rest of the conversation.

If you believe the person you are coaching has some experiences to draw from in seeking a resolution to the issue presented, then the focus needs to move away from the external problem and onto the person. Remember, your clients are smart and resourceful. They need you to help them discern what is getting in the way of their knowing or committing to what needs to happen next. Is it a pattern of thinking, a fear hidden behind cynicism, or an inherited belief that hasn't been examined? Your job is to expand your clients' awareness to see how they might relate to the situation differently.

> You want your clients to think more broadly for themselves. You facilitate this process.

Using masterful coaching techniques that challenge and disturb habitual thought patterns is *developmental* (expanding clients' perspective) instead of *operational* (exploring what didn't work and how to fix it). The conversations may feel uncomfortable, but the outcomes are remarkable. You spark more activity in your clients' brains. The changes in their beliefs and behaviors that occur when you focus on their thinking instead of just options and consequences are enduring yet adaptable. The changes that occur today are accessible to expand or change again in the future as circumstances shift around them. In chapter 8, you will learn more about how to hold a safe space for clients to be vulnerable with you while keeping them focused on the outcomes.

SUPPORTING VERSUS CHALLENGING CLIENTS

Many coaches struggle with shifting focus from the problem to the human. Both coaches and clients are more comfortable focusing on the external problem. Coaches might ask important questions to help clients analyze their perception of the situation, including what factors are making the dilemma difficult for them to resolve. Some may even coach clients to focus on their strengths to help find a solution, dipping into the realm of coaching the person instead of the problem.

These approaches are useful, but they are not enough. They allow coaches to avoid challenging clients' beliefs and thought patterns. This may keep the conversation comfortable, but it prolongs self-denial, especially when dealing with a strong ego.

Clients with years of experience in their roles like to fall back on what they know, protecting their ideas instead of opening up to new ones. Intelligent people know their strength is in how well they think. They wholeheartedly believe their rationalizations are truths. They protect their opinions as solid facts.

To be open to learning, clients must experience a moment of uncertainty. Doubt prompts people to contemplate their beliefs and motivations. Clients may get defensive, even angry, as they teeter on the edge of a cliff, hanging on to their perceptions. If you calmly maintain the balance between caring and patiently staying with the inquiry, they might let go. They will often pause in the space of not knowing what is true anymore. Generally, this break in knowing is short-lived as the fresh perspective becomes clear.

Case Study

I was coaching the leader of a division in a multinational corporation composed of an administrative base and service divisions. Many of the divisions were once separate companies, acquired by and merged into the parent company. My client's division was one of the acquired companies. He led his team well through the transition. The following year, his division was the top revenue producer for the corporation. Two years later, after a series of decisions by the parent organization, my client's division was struggling to meet its goals.

Our third session started with my client telling me his division was for sale. He started with his usual report of how the members of his leadership team were behaving and who was causing him the most trouble. I asked if he wanted to dig deeper into the motivations of his most difficult leader because not much had changed since the last session.

With some irritation, he said, "I'm doing my best here, but they've put me out on a limb and keep sawing away at the branch."

I said, "I get you are doing your best to keep your limb from crashing. You're committed to leading your organization through this transition no matter the difficulties you face. Persistence is one of your strongest values; it's who you are even when your parent company doesn't include you in the bigger decisions."

"Right, and I'm trying to protect what we have so there is something left to sell."

I asked him if he was doing everything in his control that he could do, including managing the members of his team.

He said, "I am, but—" he paused before speaking barely above a whisper—"my best leaders keep asking me if they should move on. It's difficult for me to answer that when I haven't answered it for myself."

"I understand," I said. "Sounds like you have a conflict about what you should advise them to do as their leader when you don't know what you will do for yourself. You are committed to being a good leader for them. Would it help to spend time getting clarity on your personal choices?"

With a sigh of relief, he agreed. He said that would help him be more resolute instead of reactive in his conversations.

We further clarified that he wanted to define the circumstances that would indicate it was time for him to go so he could quit speculating about "what if" scenarios. I said it sounded like he wanted to define *the tipping point*. The session shifted from external dilemmas he had already thought through to his own ambivalence around resigning, which was causing him more tension than he needed in this critical time.

My next question was, "What is making you stay other than your loyalty to your team and your desire to beat the odds?"

He went silent for a long time before he said, "I'm not sure there is anywhere I can go." Again, our session shifted to focus on his beliefs about his future. He admitted thinking he was too old for anyone to consider him to lead a company. This revelation opened the door to some possibilities he hadn't considered because he was stuck in his story about his age. Once we uncovered the belief that was causing his anxiety about pushing his team to produce, his tension subsided. He was then better able to define the tipping point that would indicate it was time to move on. He also knew what he needed to do until the tipping point occurred.

I wasn't coaching my client to leave his company. I was coaching him to be more resolute instead of reactive. At the end of the session, he said being clear about his tipping point helped him feel more confident about his decisions and interactions.

Most strong-willed clients respect someone who stands up to their resistance. Even when my clients describe me as pushy and relentless, they always end by saying I make them do what's right. I'm not happy with their saying I make them do anything, but I appreciate their way of accepting their minds being changed in the process. I also think they are acknowledging we are partners on this journey. My willingness to challenge my clients' thinking, knowing they can cut through the clutter and see the way to a solution with coaching, creates relationships of mutual respect.

You can't avoid causing unease with your observations and questions if you want people to see the world around them in a more expansive way. When you coach people to see their blocks and biases instead of sorting through problems and options, discomfort is likely to occur before the breakthrough awareness comes to light. Clients' anxiety or embarrassment is often a result of realizing they avoided a truth that was in their face all along. This tension means the coaching is working! Keep coaching the person, not the problem, and the right criteria for making critical decisions and next-step actions will become clear.

Novelist Paul Murray said, "If it's a choice between a difficult truth and a simple lie, people will take the lie every time."[1] The truth often hurts before it sets you free. In part III, you will learn the mental habits needed to gracefully hold the space for transformational coaching to transpire regardless of your clients' emotional reactions.

Coaching the person instead of the problem can be called *awareness-based coaching* to differentiate it from *solution-focused coaching*. The focus of coaching is on identifying beliefs behind opinions and actions and on fears and conflicting values causing dissonance and confusion. You want the shifts to be made at the identity level instead of just trying to alter activity.

Coaching is often supportive and encouraging; it can also be uncomfortably disruptive. You must be willing to challenge interpretations, test assumptions, and notice emotional shifts so your clients learn something new instead of just reordering the thoughts they already had.

Three Tips for Focusing on the Person, Not the Problem

Sometimes clients feel you are more annoying than helpful when trying to shift from the problem to the person. You might also need more than one session to establish the trust necessary for clients to let you in. Use the following tips to establish the rapport necessary to effectively shift from focusing on the external problem to coaching the person to find a way forward:

1. *Set the expectation for coaching.* You and your clients need to have similar expectations for what coaching sessions will look like. When you first agree with clients to be their coach, let them know you will not be their advisor. You are there to be their thinking partner to sort through what is creating uncertainty around handling an issue or deciding a way forward. You might provide facts or remind them of past issues they faced that could relate to the moment, but you will act as a confidant to help them explore perceptions and alternatives in the present. You might give reading homework or tasks to complete to aid them between sessions, but they shouldn't expect you to tell them what to do with what they learn.

2. *Maintain your belief in the client's capabilities.* Your intention for coaching must start with your belief about your clients' potential to solve the problem. You are there to help people see a way forward they couldn't see on their own. You are curious about what they want to achieve and what is stopping them from realizing this outcome. You wonder what is getting in the way and what they need to move forward. You recognize your urge to give advice when you judge their pool of knowledge and experience as inadequate. You breathe and let go of this urge as you remember your clients are creative and resourceful.

When clients know you believe in their capabilities and you are there to help them discover their best answers, they will be willing to accept the discomfort of vulnerability when admitting to their gaps, biases, and fears. Your beliefs about your clients create the conditions for learning to occur.

3. *Know the right time to shift from clarifying the problem to coaching the person in front of you.* Once you clarify a possible outcome for the coaching session—what clients want to achieve in your time together—you may ease into coaching by seeking to discover what options are possible, what they have already tried, and what they have considered doing but didn't. Often, exploring what they didn't do will reveal what is at the source of their hesitation. Most likely, the competent people you are speaking to need to expand their limiting views of what is right and wrong and what "shoulds" are directing their behavior based on what others expect or judge. They might need to unearth how a fear of failure or a skewed sense of obligation is limiting their perspective. They might also need a boost in confidence to do what they have already decided to do. If they are willing to explore what they personally need to resolve, you can shift the focus from the problem to the person. This is when they realize that without the mental distractions, they knew the right thing to do all along.

CHAPTER 4

ACTIVE REPLAY

Playing Back the Pivotal Pieces for Review

An experience makes its appearance only when it is being said.

—HANNAH ARENDT

WHEN WE USE reflective statements, we act as a dynamic mirror where clients can more objectively view their behavioral motivations and limiting beliefs. The recognition of these can be jarring. Using reflective statements is also the best way to prompt clients to think about what they are willing to do now that they better understand what needs to be resolved.

My first job after earning my master's degree in broadcast communication arts was as the audio visual coordinator for a psychiatric hospital corporation. I was in charge of setting up the television sets, video players, and film projectors. I also operated the video recording equipment if there was a medical need to record a patient.

I was disappointed with the menial work I was doing after completing an advanced degree. While looking for a more fulfilling job, I was given an assignment that turned out to be one of the most fascinating experiences of my life.

My master's thesis explored the effects video feedback had on a person's self-esteem. First, I videotaped individuals talking about a topic. After I watched the replay with each person and we talked about what they would do differently to improve their presentation skills, they were given a few days to rehearse before I taped them again. We repeated this routine one more time, for a total of adding up to three recording and replay sessions per person.

I used an assessment to measure people's self-esteem before and after the three sessions. My subjects were drug addicts and prison inmates as well as randomly selected graduate students to balance out the measures. After the third recording, the average measures spiked upward, demonstrating improvement, especially in self-awareness and confidence.

I shared my research with a psychiatric nurse who was looking for educational programs to show to her anorexic patients. She told me when her patients looked in a mirror, they only saw themselves as fat. She didn't think the use of video would make a difference, but she said it would be interesting to try. She asked her attending psychiatrist if he felt there would be any harm in trying my process with the patients. He encouraged the experiment if he could to be present at the recordings.

The results in one session were amazing. The patients gasped as they viewed themselves on video. For the first time, they saw how ghostly thin they had become. They noticed physical disfiguration and skin problems they couldn't see before.

Although they couldn't see the truth in a static mirror, the patients saw the decimation of their bodies when they watched themselves on video replay. This *active replay* process opened the door to more treatment options.

What is commonly referred to as *mirroring skills* in coaching replicates the effect of video replay. Playing back your clients' words and expressions and then asking a question that arises from your curiosity effectively provokes self-reflection. Yet unlike a mirror, you aren't providing static replications. Your reflective statements and questions provide an active replay of not just their behaviors but also the beliefs, fears, disappointments, betrayals, conflicts of values, and desires prompting their actions.

Two skills are important in the practice of active replay: (1) summarizing key points the client said and (2) noticing emotional shifts without interpreting the meaning. Summarizing and sharing the emotions you notice include the subskills described in this chapter. Pairing these practices with clarifying and exploratory questions creates inquiry. Your exploration goes deeper into the sources of clients' thought formation. The insights clients gain move them forward.

SUMMARIZING

Although summarizing may seem simplistic, the effects are powerful. When people hear their own words spoken, their ideas and beliefs are laid out in front of them to examine. They then go inward to reflect. From this vantage point, they glimpse what was a blind spot or see the inaccuracies in a belief. They are likely to pause, and possibly gasp, as the brain reorders, rewires, and formulates a new perspective to make meaning of what they now perceive.

The intent of summarizing is not to memorize and then parrot back what clients say. The aim is to help them objectively observe their stories and how they are telling them. When they hear themselves think, they can see their limited appraisal of actions, events, and options.

The practice of summarizing includes three skills: (1) recapping, (2) paraphrasing, and (3) encapsulating. You will often follow up summarizing statements with a question to confirm the accuracy of your words or the impact on the direction of the conversation, such as "How is this conflict affecting your ability to achieve your goal?" A good use of reflective inquiry is to summarize so clients hear their thoughts and then provoke examination with a question.

Recapping

One of my favorite phrases in coaching is, "So, you are telling me . . ." Then I restate the issue, problem, or outcome expressed and the key factors the client says is making it difficult to take action. The client will either agree or correct my perception without my asking a question.

Although you are highlighting, don't leave out a jarring detail. Often a side comment expressed with a shift in emotion reveals the big belief that is creating the client's block.

Case Study

My client was describing her disappointment with her husband for remaining in a night shift job for five years. She thought they agreed he would seek a day job when they had a child; they now had two children. He deflected her attempts to discuss this possibility.

I recapped by saying, "I hear that you want your husband to seek a new job, but he's not interested in having this conversation with you." She agreed. I then asked what *deflect* looked like. I wanted to better understand what was making the conversation difficult for her to initiate.

She said, "A year ago, I tried to talk about his getting a new job. He threw up a wall so big I'm scared to bring it up again. Now we don't talk much about anything important. We spend little time together. When our time at home overlaps, he's playing on his phone. I don't know how to get in."

I said, "I see. You want your husband to seek a new job, but his avoidance of this topic and your fear of his rejecting the conversation if you bring it up again is creating distance in your relationship. When you stressed the words 'threw up a wall so big,' that felt like the tipping point for you."

Her anger melted to sadness. After a long pause and a soft yes, I invited her to choose the direction of our coaching. "Do you want to look at ways of effectively approaching a conversation about his job seeking or look at how to break down the wall between you?" She chose finding a way to return to a relationship with no walls.

When recapping, use the words clients give you. Receive what they say so you can play it back to them. Include the emotions they use to stress their desires and irritations. Don't analyze the meaning. You miss key points when you start to think about what they are saying. Thinking is the enemy of the coach.

RECAPPING TO CLARIFY

Recapping helps you stay focused on sorting out the client's perception of the situation beyond the initial story. Too often, coaches hear the story and think they have the full picture. When you say, "Let me see if I understand your position" and then share the dilemma the client posed, you clarify the starting point for both you and the client. Usually, clients will add important details after they hear your summary. They also feel you are listening and present.

As you clarify, your questions should help reveal how clients feel about extenuating factors. Stay curious to discover what is most important to them, how long they have been ruminating on the situation without taking action, if something is driving a sense of urgency to act now, and what actions they have already taken that have helped or hindered their progress. Short summaries followed by questions lay out the narrative for clients cleanly and comprehensively in a way they can't do for themselves.

Be sure to note any statements they make starting with "I want" or "I need." Explore the importance of their wants and needs and the cost of not realizing them. You also want to know if they believe their desires are achievable. Then, are they willing to do what it takes to get what they want and need?

Be patient when recapping and clarifying. When you help clients crystallize the picture of what they really want to happen, what follows in the coaching will be both easier and beneficial.

RECAPPING TO RECOGNIZE CONFLICTS AND CONTRADICTIONS

Clients are often stuck when what they want conflicts with what they should or are expected to do. They might show increasing frustration or anxiety as you clarify the two positions.

Case Study

I was coaching a woman who wanted to discover how she could enjoy her work more. She said her job had become easy with no challenge. She wanted to start a new project, but the growth of the company was causing "stupid internal conflicts" that took up her time. She couldn't see a way out of this predicament. She often misplaced her anger on her family.

I recapped how the "stupid" conflicts were stopping her from enjoying her work and causing stress at home. She argued the job was good, it paid well, and it used her skills; the company was growing; and her family benefited in many ways by her staying. I summarized these reasons for staying in her job and shared that she had tensed up as she spoke them. It felt as if she was irritated with me or the coaching.

She blurted out, "Am I wrong for wanting to go? Everyone is envious of my position. It supports my family well. Who knows what will happen if I leave?"

I said, "Yes, who knows what will happen if you leave? You want to go, but everyone around you thinks you should stay."

She stared blankly at me. I stayed silent. Finally, she said, "I should be grateful, but I don't feel that way."

I said, "It sounds like your desires are in conflict with what you think you *should* do, that you are wrong and bad for wanting to go." She nodded in agreement. I asked her to weigh her desire to leave against the reasons for staying, assessing which option was most important to her at that moment.

I acknowledged how quickly and adamantly she responded and said, "Knowing you want to go, would you be willing to more deeply explore the impact of your choice, how much it really makes you wrong and bad?"

She quickly said, "I want to go."

The session didn't end with a decision. She said she had to think about it more. Two hours later, she sent me an email: "I am free to leave if I choose to. Thank you."

The session was successful because it gave the client clarity on who was making her choices for her. She was less paralyzed. She gained more ideas on how to talk with her family and detach from the opinions of people who were less important to listen to. She could now better plan her next steps, separating the unknown from the exciting possibilities.

Notice whenever your clients use the word *but* when you point out an apparent conflict, especially if their emotions demonstrate a preference for one option over another. Don't push them to choose. Help them see that they might have more options or actions to take than just the two they are considering right now.

Case Study

I had a client who decided to sell his business, but in each of our bimonthly sessions, he presented a new drama that delayed the sale. After two months of working through these events, I reflected the fact that a continuous string of events kept him from reaching his goal. I asked him if it was okay for him to make a choice—to sell or not. He said he hadn't considered not selling. He needed time to think about it.

Two days later, he called to tell me he didn't want to sell after all. He loved his "work family." He enjoyed providing a great workplace for his employees. His answer felt resolute; it did not seem like just an excuse to avoid change.

I acknowledged his courage.

Once he made his choice, he realized how delegating more responsibilities would give him the freedom to do some of the activities he thought he could do only if he sold his company.

> When there is a conflict of values, people feel stuck in the middle. Summarizing conflicts in coaching gives clients both the clarity and confidence to choose what to do next.

Be careful not to judge which is your clients' best option. Accept whatever your clients decide is right for them in this moment.

Paraphrasing

In the case study of the client who wanted to leave her job but felt others were judging her decision as wrong, I used the words *wrong* and *bad* to clarify her conflict. She used the word *wrong*; I added the word *bad* to check on the depth of her fear. It is easier to live with wrong decisions than ones that hurt others. I offered her the words *wrong* and *bad* based on her emotions. Although she expressed disdain when describing the stupid conflicts she had to deal with at work, her guilt seeped out when talking about how people would judge her decision to leave. She wasn't just considering a right or wrong decision; she felt she would be judged as good or bad based on what she chose to do.

Paraphrasing helps clients assess the meaning of their words and emotions. We restate what we hear in a slightly different form to help them surface and explore their beliefs.

Paraphrasing is an offer; clients can accept your words or not. If they don't agree, it's likely they will offer an alternative clarifier.

You will be interjecting an interpretation of their words when paraphrasing. Be careful to base your version on what they said. If you are guessing what they are facing based on your own experiences, you have stepped into judgment instead of reflection.

Knowing if you are paraphrasing or judging can be difficult to discern in real time. If you are working on this skill, a good practice is to get permission from your clients to record your sessions to review and then erase. When you hear yourself paraphrase, ask what statements your client made that led to your choice of words. Did your words lead to clarity, or did you lead your client to accept a definition of the situation based on your own experiences? As best you can, make sure your paraphrase is an alternative statement of what was said, not your opinion about what the client shared.

Another form of paraphrasing is to use a metaphor. You use a metaphor to paint a picture of what the client is telling you in a different context connected by meaning. For example, when a leader is describing why she doesn't trust her employees enough to delegate responsibility to them, you might say, "Sounds like you keep pruning your plants instead of trusting the teenager next door to do the job."

If the client agrees with the representation, you can then explore what beliefs underlie the picture. In the delegation example, you would explore the comparison between the leader's beliefs about the inadequacies of her employees and the teenager next door. You might find out her team is new and she has no experience to draw from. In this case, delegation needs to start with training. Or you might find your client's judgments of the inadequacies of others are too harsh. This may lead to the fears that stop the leader from delegating. Metaphor is a great clarifier.

Encapsulating

Sometimes you can capture the major elements of a client story in just a few words. You use a phrase or even one word to name the client's experience. This practice includes labeling, bottom lining, and drawing distinctions.

LABELING

When labeling clients' experience, you are offering a title for their story. You can grab a few words they used when telling their story, such as "It's a huge unknown" or "No trust." You can also use a short metaphor, such as "Sounds like you are drowning" or "Sounds like you are pushing a huge rock up a hill" or "Sounds like you've lost sight of the finish line." If clients simply agree with no explanation, you can follow up by asking, "What does this picture mean to your achieving what you said you wanted from this session?"

Case Study

I was coaching a leader who wanted to explore why he was being indecisive about accepting an attractive job offer from a company in a country he would like to live in. His history included three job shifts in another industry. After joining a company, he quickly added new products that increased its revenue dramatically and then moved on to a new company in the same industry.

His current job was his first in a new industry. He was grateful the CEO trusted his talents. The CEO also gave him a senior

---

leadership position. He was learning a lot as a leader beyond his gifts in innovation and implementation. But the job offer he was considering would be good for his family as well as test his skills.

I said, "Sounds like there's some loyalty."

"Yes!" he said. "That's it! Loyalty—I never felt that before. That's why it was easier for me to leave jobs before now."

The conversation shifted to his exploring if loyalty was a block or a benefit. He decided to stay longer in his position as he liked expanding his role as a leader.

The one word—*loyalty*—summed up his dilemma. The label gave him the clarity he needed to evaluate his conflict.

BOTTOM LINING

Bottom lining helps clients isolate what needs to be resolved to achieve their desired outcome. They often agree on what they want but then declare all the reasons why they can't move forward. When you summarize their reasons, they add to the list. The conversation then runs in circles.

Listen for the word *but*. The word *but* signals that their brain is conjuring up excuses for not acting. Bring the conversation back to the statement made before the *but* to see if, bottom line, that action is what they want to take if it is worth the risk.

Bottom lining is also used to discern likely from not-so-likely consequences of taking a risk. For example, after clients list all the bad things that could happen, you might say, "Bottom line, you want to find a new job, but three things could make this move difficult at this time." From this perspective, they can better examine what is keeping them from acting now.

> Bottom-line statements help clients see
> through the fog of fear.

Bottom lining can also be used to summarize beliefs and insights.

Case Study

I had a client who couldn't seem to find the right time to ask her boss to broaden her responsibilities. She always had a good excuse for not making the request.

I asked, "Bottom line, what is the worst thing that could happen if you ask for what you want?" She said she was afraid her boss might see her as wanting his job. I said, "You see your boss in an adversarial position. What makes you think he will respond this way to your request?" She admitted he probably wouldn't respond so negatively. She also said she would make sure her request didn't feel like a threat.

This led me to say, "That felt easy. What's the real risk you are facing?"

She blurted out, "What if I'm not up to taking on more?"

I said, "So bottom line, your hesitation is based on your fear of failure, not on how your boss might react." She agreed.

I asked if she had a picture of what success might look like in the next step of her career. She easily described this picture. I asked if she wanted to shift the focus of the coaching session to how she might achieve the success she envisioned. She then identified the gaps in her skills and knowledge, which led her to determine her developmental needs. In the end, my client found no good reason for not setting a date to talk with her boss about her future.

The doubt that keeps people from moving forward is often steeped in fears of feeling humiliated and embarrassed. They don't want to look stupid, be judged as incompetent in a role such as a leader or parent, or be rejected for making a change. They spend more time defending inaction than planning actions to take.

Concisely summarizing the points clients make helps them assess the likelihood of the loss they fear. They rise above their defenses. They can also see what they would do next if what they fear comes to pass.

I often follow up the bottom-line statement with the question, "What would you do if you had nothing to worry about, if no *buts* existed?" The question helps not only clarify what they truly want to do but also to weaken the impact of their fears.

DRAWING DISTINCTIONS

One of my favorite practices is drawing distinctions to help clarify what a person wants or what needs to be resolved. For example, I had a client who wanted to be more resilient but feared her brain was getting stale with age. She wasn't taking action as quickly as she did when she started her career. To clarify what she thought she was losing, I said, "I hear two things. You don't take action quickly and you don't see options quickly. Which is the bigger problem: you aren't as bold as you were when you were younger, or you aren't as clever as you once were when seeking solutions?" She said she wasn't as clever, which led us to explore how she faces issues differently today than years ago.

She finally said, "I'm just tired."

I asked, "Are you tired of the work you are doing, or is it that you have so much to do, you are physically drained?" She chose the latter definition. This led her to talk about her lack of self-care, which led to a new outcome to work on for our coaching session.

Other common distinctions include comparing clients' passion to their level of joy for their current commitments, exploring their self-imposed standards of excellence versus their need for perfection, and how quality versus quantity factor into their measures of success. You can also help clients process the meaning of their words, such as when they say, "I'm fed up with their behavior" and you ask, "What does *fed up* mean: you are out of options to solve the problem or you are angry with their behavior?" The clarification shifts clients to consider what they really want to resolve.

When you hear a conflict of desires or values, you can better frame the options by asking, "Are your two options in conflict with each other, or could you achieve a little more of both?" Some examples include

+ A client who wants to take a new job but doesn't want to disrupt his family's routine
+ A client who wants to spend more time with her family but wants more recognition for her contributions at work
+ A client who likes helping others yet wants more time to himself
+ A client who loves the sense of accomplishment her work provides but feels it is time to experience life differently

Drawing distinctions is a great way to clarify where clients are stuck in their thinking. Distinctions clarify what clients think and feel. They crystalize what needs to be resolved to move forward. They can pinpoint conflicts of values to better explore options. Use distinctions to help clients cut through confusion. The conversation will move forward more quickly.

PAIRING SUMMARIZING WITH QUESTIONS

Once you summarize by recapping, paraphrasing, and encapsulating what clients offer in the conversation, you can follow up your statement with a question. The question will come from your curiosity about how they see the situation from the perspective you offered. Even closed questions that follow your summaries—such as "Is this correct?" or "Is this what bothers you most?"—can be powerful clarifiers. You don't have to spend time remembering coaching questions that have worked before. The questions will emerge from the reflection you share.

Three Tips for Summarizing

When your clients are stuck seeing no resolution to their predicaments, they get lost trying to explain their perspective. Summarizing is a way to help them break through the fog to see the path they are on. With increased clarity, they are better able to recognize their blocks and options. Use the following tips to succinctly reflect your clients' experience to help them objectively observe their situation:

1. *Use your clients' words when recapping or encapsulating the outcome they want and the factors they feel are delaying their movement.* Then ask them to explain what their key words mean. Key words include their interpretation (the why) of their actions; points they make following the word *really,* such as "What I really want . . ." or "What the issue really is . . ."; and emotionally charged phrases.

2. *Use metaphors to paraphrase how clients are reacting to a situation.* Paint a picture in a different context that has the same meaning, such as "It feels you are carrying the world on your shoulders,"

"You seem to be rowing upstream," or "You are surrounded by vultures." Follow up with questions to surface the underlying beliefs, assumptions, and fears that are framing their perception.

3. *Cut through excuses and unnecessary backstory details by bottom lining what you hear is the outcome they want and the biggest block to achieving it.* If they agree, you can use distinctions to further clarify what needs to be resolved, such as asking, "Do you want this . . . or this . . . ?" or "Are you more afraid of losing something you care about or of what you will have to do if you go for your dreams?" Bottom lining and drawing distinctions clarify client thinking, allowing them to get to solutions quicker.

NOTICING EMOTIONAL SHIFTS

People don't always tell the truth.

That does not mean they are intentionally lying or withholding information. They often don't know how to articulate what they are feeling and why. They might be uncomfortable sharing a strong opinion if they don't know how you will react. They may avoid disclosing an embarrassing thought or action.

Yet emotions, hesitations, and exaggerations can reveal what your clients need to resolve before they can decide what to do next. You can help them bring what is difficult to articulate to the surface by offering your observation of emotional shifts in their expressions.

When I summarize what people tell me and ask if what I said best describes what is going on, or I list the different problems they told me they want to address and ask which one is most important, *they stop and think about their thinking.* When I notice and share a shift in their emotions, *they stop and think about their feelings.* Exploring emotions can be more powerful than exploring thoughts when seeking to identify beliefs, conflicts, or fears that are deterring forward movement.

When you actively replay an expressed emotion, you open the door to discuss dilemmas in a way your clients would or could not do in conversations outside of coaching. For example, you might notice when they do the following:

+ Look down or away as they change their tone of voice
+ Hesitate or become silent
+ Get louder or more animated
+ Stress the words *always* or *never* when describing how they interpret other people's intentions or behavior
+ Use the word *really* accompanied by a heightened tone that accentuates a declaration, such as "What I *really* want" or "What I *really* can't stand"

You recognize and share the emotional reactions you notice without attempting to fix or soothe clients' experience. Then, coming from a place of not knowing, you use compassionate curiosity to explore what might be the beliefs, fears, doubts, or conflicts that triggered the expression.

When you have compassionate curiosity, you accept what your clients feel without judgment. You don't use questions to change their feelings. You question the source of their reactions to understand the relationship of an emotion to their desired outcome.

After you share the shift you notice, you might ask what the expression means to them to see if the reflection triggers an insight. If they are blankly silent, you might pause as they process the reflection. If they hesitate to talk, ask if they wouldn't mind sharing their thoughts. As they attempt to explain what their reaction meant, use your summarizing skills to connect their emotions to the story they shared when defining their dilemma.

> When we come to understand our emotional reactions, we better understand ourselves.

Noticing emotional shifts is a powerful yet underused coaching skill. I wrote *The Discomfort Zone* as a result of watching coaches miss or refuse to comment on what appeared to be negative emotions. They were adept at sharing when clients expressed enthusiasm, passion, or relief but not the darker emotions such as anger, cynicism, or guilt. Or coaches jumped in with a suggestion to ease the pain they noticed. Their sympathy overrode their empathy. Unfortunately, their attempts to make their clients feel better didn't allow their clients to work through their emotions to a better understanding. Some clients felt bad for reacting.

> When you interrupt the coaching to render aid, clients no longer feel they can fully express themselves with you.

Appreciating Emotions as Important to Growth

Most of us were brought up to believe some emotions are negative and bad.

I like feeling happy as much as anyone. I'm more productive when my mood is bright. I'm easier to be with when I'm hopeful about tomorrow.

I have also made big changes in my life through the power of my anger, realized the depth of my courage when feeling my fear, and learned what is important in life from sorrow.

You need to give your clients a safe space to shed their tears, allow them to feel angry and hurt, and accept when they don't trust anyone, including you, in the moment. You need to affirm the doubtful critic and the disappointed visionary without giving them false hope. Even when you have lived your clients' story, you can show you care without holding their hand.

> When you deprive clients from feeling,
> you stunt their growth.

Trying to make them feel better, even running to get a tissue for a crier, will negatively affect the coaching no matter the value of your intention. They might feel less understood or enfeebled when you interrupt to save them. The response you believe is "being supportive" could damage their willingness to fully express themselves to you.

Clients don't need you to cheer them up. They want you to acknowledge they are okay no matter what they feel. This total acceptance encourages them to talk about their feelings so they can better understand them. Understanding the source of their emotions weakens the impact on their thinking. They are better able to recognize what is now possible or what they know they must do. They can use what they learn from their emotional reactions to make their delayed decisions.

Using Nonreactive Empathy

When with others, you are picking up emotional signals that you then interpret through the lens of your experiences. Your life experiences give you the capacity for empathy where you might understand the source of their emotional reactions. However, recognizing an emotional shift and understanding why others feel the way they do are not the same.

Empathy is subjective. When you interpret why people feel the way they do, your opinion might be correct or not. The visceral reaction you have when sensing the emotions of others is real. Your understanding of the source may or may not be accurate.

Case Study

I was coaching a manager who was anxious about an upcoming conversation with an employee whose performance as a supervisor was hurting the team. The manager hoped the conversation would convince his employee to readily accept a demotion, but he worried she would quit. As we talked through possible approaches, his frustration grew. Finally, he lowered his head and muttered, "But I thought she'd be the one." Then he lifted his head and continued to talk about her volatility.

I not only noticed the shift in his posture and voice but also felt a pain in my chest when he said, "I thought she'd be the one." I said, "Hold on. Can we go back to something you just said, when you lowered your head and voice? Something about her being the one. You got quiet, as if you were sad."

He let out a deep breath and said, "More embarrassed than sad. It might be my fault. I might have promoted her too soon."

"Can we talk about that and how that might play into your conversation with her?"

He frowned and said, "Of course." My observations allowed him to face his fear of her judging him as a bad leader. After looking into this belief and accepting he made a mistake, the conversation shifted to how he might share his revelation with her, hoping she would step back to get the training and mentoring she needed to succeed as a supervisor when she felt ready. He still believed in her potential.

Share the emotional shifts you notice in your clients. Wait for a response or ask what they think the expression means. Does their excitement represent something of value to them? Do they know where their doubt is coming from? If you have an inkling about what caused the shift, offer an idea or a distraction with no attachment to being right. Is their frustration based on their current work assignments or the lack of a path forward in the future? Are they angry about a decision that was made without them, or are they angry they haven't spoken up? Let your clients determine the interpretation of their reaction. Your options will help them think more deeply about their thoughts and feelings, even if their interpretation is different from yours. If they correct you, they clarify the source of their feelings for themselves.

> Trust your ability to feel emotional shifts in your clients; then use your curiosity to explore what triggered the reaction.

If their experience reminds you of one of your own, keep your story to yourself. When you tell them you have felt the same way in the past, you jump out of coaching and into fixing.

If you want your clients to feel comfortable being vulnerable with you, you need to let your reactions to their emotions fade away. You create a safe space for the conversation to unfold by caring and feeling compassionately curious. Then you can identify and understand what they feel, not feel it with them.

> Humans desire to be seen beyond their words. Recognizing emotional shifts with compassionate curiosity demonstrates you care.

Even at work, most people long for others to understand how they feel, the foundation of empathy. Clients want you to sense their discomfort or distress, especially when they struggle with articulating the emotions they are experiencing. They also might hope you have a compassionate response to their revelation. Ask them how their emotions are impacting their desired outcome. Seek to discover if they want to work through their emotions or they just need a safe place to talk.

Can Too Much Empathy Be Bad?

In my emotional intelligence and coaching skills classes, I am often asked if too much empathy can be bad. If you embody the emotions you pick up from others, the answer could be yes. If you instead notice and release the emotions in your body so you can hold the space for others to safely express themselves, the answer is no.

Your capacity to experience empathy is not the same as emotional contagion, where you take on the emotions of another. Most people long to feel seen, heard, and valued no matter what they express. They want to feel safe enough to express themselves without feeling judged. They don't need you to feel sad, stressed, angry, or anxious with them.

If you take on their emotions beyond your initial sense of their reactions, they might feel they have to take care of you. They might feel guilty or sorry for upsetting you. Noticing clients' emotional reactions is an instantaneous response you share and then release in a noncritical way.[1] If you felt their emotion, you relax your body and let the emotion subside as you return to being fully present with your clients. If you let these emotions sit in your body, your body and mind will be emotionally hijacked.

Unbridled emotional contagion can lead to concentrations of the stress hormone cortisol, which makes it difficult to release the emotions.[2] Taking on other people's feelings in coaching can break the bond of trust you were hoping to strengthen. You may feel responsible for relieving their pain. You quit coaching as you jump in to fix their problems to make them feel better. You do this to make yourself feel better too.

> You appreciate and encourage expression in others by observing their emotional reactions, sensing the experience in your own body, sharing what you witness and sense, and then letting the emotions go.

Noticing emotional expressions and shifts without letting your own emotions get in the way encourages clients' exploration. The intensity of their emotions subsides. They can think more clearly about their thinking. The coaching can more smoothly move forward.

Three Tips for Noticing Emotional Shifts

Reflecting emotional shifts can be powerful as well as intimidating for both coach and client. Coaches need to manage their discomfort when noticing their clients' emotional reactions to objectively share their observations. Then, although sharing emotional shifts can provoke a new awareness, clients often react with a strong emotion before the insight emerges. Use the following tips to effectively reflect your clients' emotional expressions:

1. *Notice shifts in clients' posture, tone of voice, facial expressions, and breathing.* Start your sentences with "I noticed . . . ," "I heard . . . ," or "I sense . . ." Offer these reflections with no

attachment to being right. Pause to let your clients process your reflection. Wait for a response or ask what they think their emotional shift meant. If they aren't sure, you might offer a possible source of their emotion based on what they previously told you. If they identify the source as different from what you offered, they will correct you, which shines a light on the emotions they couldn't see before. If they are hesitant to respond, Ron Carucci suggests using statements like "Tell me how I should interpret your silence" and "It seems that what I just said made you think about something else. Would you share that with me?"[3] Don't push if they aren't ready to talk about how they feel. The awareness that is emerging may need time to gestate.

2. *Be receptive to their experience, no matter what they say and express.* Your clients need to feel safe from judgment to express themselves freely. If their emotions make you uncomfortable, breathe and release the tension so you can stay present and open. If your body tightens up with judgment due to your own biases, slowly exhale while you clear your mind. Remind yourself to warmly regard the humans sitting in front of you who are trusting you to help them solve a dilemma. You don't need to mentally or physically detach from them unless you sense a real threat of physical harm.

3. *Practice curiosity.* Discover what the emotion of curiosity feels like in your brain and body. Then, if you become uncomfortable with your clients' expression—when you move from empathy to sympathy where you feel bad for them or when you take on their emotions as your own—shift to feeling curious so you can resume coaching.

CHAPTER 5

BRAIN HACKING

Finding the Treasures in the Box

*The very moments . . . we want
people to think outside the box,
they can't even see the box.*

—RICHARD BOYATZIS

IN THE MIDDLE of my brain is a box full of stories I use to navigate each day of my life (fig. 1). The frame of the box has thickened through the years, protecting my stories and points of view from outside disruption. From the moment I wake up, I know who I am and what I'm supposed to do based on the stories that guide me. I have an "I always wake up early" story I can't seem to change. I hold my "morning exercise routine" story as sacred for upholding my quality of life at my age. I am open-minded, willing to accept when I judge others incorrectly, but I wrote this book believing my views around coaching are solid. When I realize I

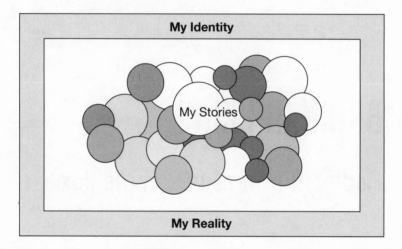

Figure 1. Box of stories.

don't have an answer, I quickly check in with my mentors, my books, and my research to maintain my "expert" story.

There is little I am uncertain about, even when uncertainty swirls around me. I'll draw on my stories to give meaning to my circumstances, calling my interpretation *the truth*. Political philosopher Hannah Arendt said, "The need of reason is not inspired by the quest for truth but by the quest for meaning. And truth and meaning are not the same."[1] The brain seeks to make meaning of events; it doesn't take time to verify the truth.

> Our frames keep us safe *and* stuck.

You have a box full of stories too. Your stories differ from mine, even if we share similar experiences.

The frame around our stories is woven from strands of our significant life experiences and learnings, forming the meaning we attach to each moment (reality) and how we define ourselves (identity). Because we need a sense of who we think we are and what we call *reality* to get out of bed in the morning, our frames are fairly solid and stable. In daily conversations, we defend our frames as right for us.

The field inside the frame is our context (fig. 2). Our contextual field holds what we believe is most important (life values) and what we need to feel good about ourselves and our relationships (social needs). Our values and needs define what we perceive as right, wrong, good, and bad in the world. Therefore, our context creates the rules we live by, with some rules being more important than others. These rules also define the standards we would like others to live up to.

Our beliefs, biases, and assumptions come from our experiences but are formed through the filter of our life values and social needs. As we experience life, we pull from our context to make meaning of our situations. The meaning then becomes our stories.

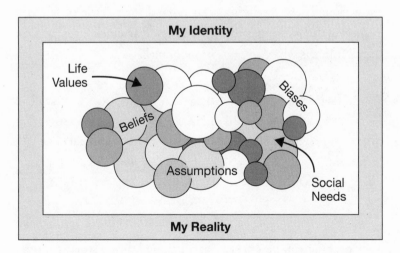

Figure 2. The contextual field inside our frame shapes our stories.

Our values and needs shape our beliefs and biases, which mix with our experiences to create stories.

Coaching is best done from the inside out. We listen to our clients' stories and coach them to examine the beliefs, biases, and assumptions holding their stories together. Coaching at this level can be what clients need to open their minds to new possibilities. When you coach them to see what beliefs and biases no longer serve them, the shift in perspective can be transformational. When the narrative of their stories shifts, they can more confidently plan, make decisions, and promise to take action.

If your clients still feel stuck or hesitant after exploring their beliefs and are willing to go deeper, look at how their life values and social needs play into their stories. The exploration can surface conflicts of values, fears, and what clients really want but have resisted articulating, leading to a new awareness and choices for action. These revelations can expand their sense of self and reality, making changes to their frames. The crack or expansion of the frame is what we call a *breakthrough*.

The frame (identity and reality), the contextual field inside the frame (values and needs), and our stories (shaped by beliefs, biases, and assumptions) dictate our thinking and actions. This is our operating system, running continuously throughout the day.

Coaching can be effective at all these levels—story, context, and frame—depending on what clients want and are ready to see.

COACHING THE STORY

Because our brains don't like uncertainty and are adept at assigning meaning to our moments, we instantly compose stories using our beliefs, biases, and assumptions. Some stories are laced with fears. Some are lined with desires and hopes. Our stories then become memories and float in the contextual field inside our frames (fig. 3). We access these narratives to give definition and direction in the moment.

We believe in the stories we tell, even though they are built on subjective elements. Jonathan Gottschall, author of *The Storytelling Animal*, says, "For humans, story is like gravity: a field of force that surrounds us and influences all of our movements. But, like gravity, story is so omnipresent that we are hardly aware of how it shapes our lives."[2] We unconsciously navigate our days based on the stories we recall.

Because of our protective instincts, we rarely evaluate and change our stories on our own. However, when someone else

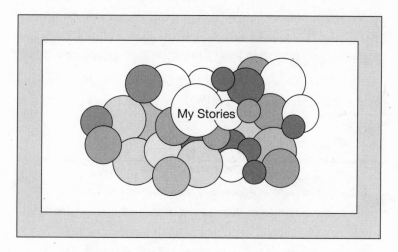

Figure 3. Stories give meaning to the moment.

summarizes, paraphrases, and repeats back to us the words we say and the pictures we draw, we are able to see our stories as if they were laid out in front of us, outside our heads.

Coaching at the story level is a good place to start. When listening to a client's story, the coach can pinpoint key beliefs holding the story together. The coach can also see and inquire about gaps in logic and unverified assumptions that paralyze action.

Without going deeply into values and needs, coaching the story can surface unsubstantiated fears and unspoken desires. Coaching the story often leads to more options for action than what clients thought they had to choose from. The verbalization might clarify the choice the client wants to make but is avoiding the discomfort of making.

> Whether your coaching goes deeper or not, coaching should start with hearing the person's story about a situation.

Examining how beliefs and assumptions are holding their stories together are the most accessible part of clients' narrative. After scrapping or modifying old beliefs and unverified assumptions, clients often feel a sense of relief. They might claim they had a breakthrough; they broke through the limits of their stories. They see a way forward with more peace of mind.

Case Study

I was coaching the vice president of a company who was preparing her team for a merger. One of her managers was not meeting deadlines for reports important to the transition process. Peers reported this manager was very negative in meetings. My client detailed everything she had done so far with her manager to figure out why she wasn't doing the reports, why she was abrasive with her peers, and what she needed to do to get on board with the transition process.

I said, "It sounds like you have done all you can to save her."

She paused, sighed, and said, "Yes, I hoped she would turn this around. I guess I should let her go."

"*Should* is an interesting word for an option you haven't taken. What does the word *should* mean to you?"

"It's the responsible choice I've been avoiding," she said. "I know I am balking. I just haven't said it out loud."

"Now that you have said it, what's different?"

"Honestly, the executives want to see if I can make tough decisions. My division will be a cornerstone for the new organization. We might even be recognized as a stand-alone business unit with our own budget and CEO. They want me to bring over the right team. I just didn't want to give up."

"What would happen if you gave up?"

"Shouldn't I be able to turn this around? Aren't I a bad leader for losing one of my people in the process?"

"But you implied you would be seen as a good leader if you let her go so you had the right team for the transition. What is the story you are telling yourself that is keeping you from letting her go?"

"That I am the super leader who can save anyone."

"So you are saying *super leader* and *tough leader* are in conflict. Like Superman and Batman. Or Superwoman. I guess you need to choose which cape you want to wear!"

She laughed and said, "Capes are so outdated!" She committed to act on her tough decision that week. Within a year, she was named CEO.

The quickest way to shift your clients' perception of a situation is to coach them to sort through the beliefs and assumptions shaping their dilemma. The clarity this coaching creates may be all they need to confidently move forward.

Beliefs and Assumptions

Offering what you hear as a belief or assumption and asking clients how they know it is true can reveal another possibility of what is true. Some assumptions were made to make sense of the circumstances but haven't been verified. Some beliefs can be seen as irrational when held out for examination. The narrative then changes, which can be enlightening and even life changing.

Case Study

In a coaching session I observed, the client stated her outcome was to feel motivated about her goals. She said she had lost her passion and life felt gray. When she was younger, she woke up eager to work on her goals. Now she was afraid she was getting old and stale.

While telling her story, she briefly mentioned the loss of her family's life savings to pay for her husband's back surgery. The coach asked if the loss meant she needed to make new goals. The client said she didn't know if she needed a new goal or just a new plan.

At first, the coach tried to explore the client's strengths and values to see if she could create a vision of a more desirable future. The client resisted, describing the hole she was living in, saying it felt like a grave. The coach asked what she was most sad about. The client said she was sad she had lost her youth.

The coach replied, "You don't seem to have the energy to create a new dream."

"No!" she said. "I want my old dream back!"

Her anger surprised both her and the coach. The coach said, "Who took it away?"

"It's not my husband's fault he needed surgery, but sometimes I'm mad about it. Then I get mad at myself for being mad. Then I don't want to do anything."

"So now you can't make your dream come true."

After a long pause, the client said, "I can, but it's like starting over. There is so much I have to redo."

"So it's not your youth you lost but the ease of living into your dream."

"I don't know if I have the energy to start over."

"Can we explore your belief around starting over?"

The client agreed. She said she really wanted the old dream, not a new one, but thought she had to give it up. Thinking she could no longer have what she had worked so hard for, plus her sense of guilt for blaming her husband, left her feeling like she was living in a grave.

The coach said, "So starting over isn't about giving up your dream but having to do more than you hoped you would have to do at your age. What about your age is stopping you now?"

"Now that we are talking about it, it's not my age. I'm still upset that things changed. Isn't that crazy? Of course, things change. I don't always get what I want."

"So what does this realization mean to you?"

The client said she didn't have to be young to start a new life chapter. It was just going to be more difficult than she had hoped it would be. With her experience, she didn't have to start all over again.

She also realized that reclaiming her dream gave her energy. Allowing herself to be angry at life was okay too. She had been taught anger was bad, especially when shown by a woman. She realized not only that her belief around the liability in expressing anger had held her back but that the suppression made her feel like she was dying. The coach then asked her how she might use her anger to reclaim her dream. She eagerly listed the many steps she would now take. She left the session feeling empowered, energized, and hopeful.

It has been said, "The smallest change in perspective can change a life." Coaching helps clients question their beliefs about current and future circumstances. A new awareness can broaden what they *believe* is possible to create and what is required to achieve what they want. This reflection can lead to an expanded or different story that changes their life choices.

Biases

Beliefs are often based in bias, both conscious (implicit) and unconscious (explicit). Bias is a tendency to stereotype and judge people or things. Biases can shield us from harm. They also distance us from others and short-circuit our empathy.

Sometimes we are conscious of our biases. We staunchly defend them, believing we are right, with or without evidence. If a bias is tied to a life value, such as the importance of having a work ethic or the need to prioritize family over work, we either expect others to believe as we do or, when motivated to understand, accept that other people have different values from us.[3]

With coaching, we hope to bring client biases to light, especially if they are hindering our clients from achieving their goals.

Clients who aspire to be good leaders, parents, or humans might be open to examining the validity of their biases. In addition to coaching, respectful dialogue among people with different perspectives can also change minds.

Derek Black, the godson of David Duke, was heir apparent to his father's white nationalism movement—until he went to college. After a series of dinners and dialogues initiated by an Orthodox Jew, Black published a letter saying, "I can't support a movement that tells me I can't be a friend to whomever I wish or that other people's races require me to think of them in a certain way or be suspicious at their advancements."[4] The dinner conversations weren't full of hate and finger-pointing. The intent of the participants was to know each other better. Friendships formed between people who once saw each other as enemies because they were open to exploring their biases.

Unconscious bias is often referred to as a blind spot. Typical unconscious biases relate to attitudes about age, race, nationality, gender, religion, and lifestyle choices. The impact of biases ranges from simply annoying others with our pet peeves and opinions to motivating us to seriously harm others. If we hold a position of power over others, we may limit their opportunities and choices based on the judgments created from our biases.

Bringing an unconscious bias to light might be enough, giving clients a chance to consider holding on or letting go. They may need time to think about the revelation, especially if they feel embarrassed or sad about their past actions. If they choose to retain their biases regardless of alternative evidence presented, they may need to consider how they will manage the impact of expecting others to have the same beliefs. They might be able to release some expectations that others think as they do; this is a good first step. Even the slow release of thinking everyone should have the same bias is a powerful transformation.

Listen for your clients' beliefs, biases, and assumptions. Offer what you perceive for their confirmation or rebuttal. Your coaching will go deeper as you explore how your clients think instead of focusing on finding solutions. Fears and unspoken desires might emerge, opening new doors where the walls seemed intact. When this happens, you become a true thinking partner.

COACHING THE CONTEXT

Our context is defined by the rules and standards that define our lives (fig. 4). To get through the day, you have a strong sense of how the world ought to work and how other people should behave. These concepts come from what we believe is most important to focus on in our lives—our values—and what we need to feel good about ourselves and our relationships—our social needs.

When coaching clients to examine the beliefs shaping their stories, you might discover the life values and social needs that formed the beliefs. Positions of power and privilege, cultural

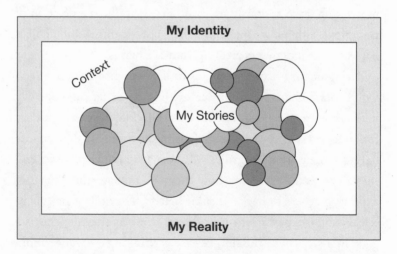

Figure 4. Our stories sit in a contextual field of life values and social needs.

norms, and things that make us happy and feel successful shape what we think is important to have. They also create judgment and fear, two emotions that keep us locked in the stories we live by.

Our brains would rather validate our values and needs than question them; questioning the rules we live by can feel scary. Psychologist Joshua Aronson said, "Fear is the enemy of curiosity."[5] Coaching can override the fear of confronting values and needs. Using reflective inquiry, we question beliefs and, as Dewey said, "In the suspense of uncertainty, we metaphorically climb a tree."[6] From this perspective, clients feel more detached when examining their thinking and they are more open to learning.

Social Needs

I laugh to myself whenever I hear someone say, "I don't like needy people." As a social animal, you have needs. The reason you are needy is because social needs fuel your drive to connect with others and flourish.

On the positive side, social needs are the drivers of success. My need for attention helps me succeed as a writer, teacher, and public speaker. My need for recognition drives my desire to do good work. My need for control helps me run a successful business.

Your needs, along with your values, mold your identity. You discovered and integrated early in life what helps you thrive. You found what enables you to be seen and recognized or what keeps you from standing out if being seen feels unsafe. You learned what you are good at that makes you feel worthwhile. As you matured, you identified what boundaries make your work and life feel comfortable, whether you hold people to these boundaries or not. Your identity includes what you think you need from other people, such as respect, recognition, a sense of order, control, being liked, or independence.

On the shadow side, the rejection or violation of a social need may trigger a range of emotions, including fear, anger, vengefulness, disappointment, frustration, and sadness. We react emotionally when we don't get what we expect. We need to examine why we expected to get our need met, and even dispute the assumptions that created what we feel is an unmet need, to be free to see what is most productive to do next.

> You may think you use logic to make decisions, when your unconscious and overriding driver is the desire to get a social need met.

When you notice your clients negatively shift when telling their story, seek to understand what social need they expected to be fulfilled or what they need but fear won't materialize. They might show resentment and judge other people's behavior as negative without evidence. Or they might give in, saying, "It will never change. I just have to live with it" or "Screw them. I'll get what I should have gotten elsewhere."

Needs are not bad. The reason we have needs is that at some point in our lives, a need served us. For example, your experiences may have taught you that success in life depends on maintaining control, establishing a sense of safety in your environment, and having people around you who appreciate your intelligence. Behavior is often motivated by getting your needs met. You are most happy when your family and colleagues meet your needs, even if just a little.

However, the more you are attached to having a need met in a situation, the more your brain will be on the lookout for people who might not give you what you need. They might even ridicule your need. When you speculate you won't get what you need, or you think you are being negatively judged for having a need, you emotionally react.

At this point, you must judge what is real about others' intentions and the impact their behavior has on you. Are they actively denying your need, or are you taking the situation too personally? You might realize their intentions were good, even if the impact was not.

Without consciously acknowledging the needs that trigger our emotional reactions, we become enslaved to the needs. On the other hand, when we honestly declare our needs—that we had expected people to treat us in a particular way and had hoped events would unfold as we had planned—we can choose to let people know what we expected from them and then ask for what we need. Or if we really didn't experience a loss, we can breathe and let the need go.

> Recognizing needs frees us to choose our reactions.

The following list includes some of the most common emotional triggers, meaning we react when we feel as though we aren't getting or will not get one of these social needs:[7]

acceptance	respect	being liked
being understood	being needed	being valued
being in control	being right	being treated fairly
attention	comfort	freedom
peacefulness	balance	consistency
order	variety	love
safety	predictability	being included
independence	new challenges	fun

The first step in helping clients articulate their needs is to notice their emotional reactions and shifts, especially if their tone turns negative. They might get angry or sad when explaining what they hoped would transpire. Listen for statements such as "They promised me," "How could they make that decision?" "He's clueless," "She did it again," or even "I'm tired" and "I'm sick of this place." Encourage your clients to discuss their feelings. What was the betrayal? What was so disrespectful? What was annoying or unbelievable? Letting clients process their emotions will help them understand the unfulfilled needs that triggered their reactions.

When they discover the unmet need, invite your clients to choose one of these options. Ask, "Can you

+ ask for what you need?" (For example, to be heard, for a little recognition, or to be included in a decision.)
+ get your need met elsewhere?"
+ learn from the experience and move on?" (For example, What do you want to develop or accept? What is based on an old story you no longer need to tell? Can you let go of something so you don't feel stuck?)

Be careful you don't judge your clients' needs. Some of these needs will mirror your own; others will not. Clients may have needs you think are trivial. These needs are important to them. Don't make light of what they need.

You are needy. I am needy. Your clients will all be needy. Our brains are often plotting to get what we need. We avoid, rebel against, or attempt to emotionally detach from those who don't give us what we need, including family. Talking about emotions and needs brings clarity on what we have to resolve to move forward.

Life Values

Your strongly held beliefs about what is most important are your values. They are the most stable elements in your contextual field. Your values direct your choices of work, friends, relationships, and a desired future. You are generally happy if you live in alignment with your values.

Some values hold more weight than others, and values can change in priority over time. Events and age will change your perspective on what you hold most dear. As I grow older, activities that improve my health hold more value. Since I have no children and my parents have passed away, my value for family has weakened and my value for friendship has increased. These days, my passion for learning is greater than the desire for winning that drove me in my twenties and thirties. Bringing values to light in a coaching conversation can help clients realize what values are growing in strength and which ones are receding.

The desired outcomes of a coaching session should reflect something your clients value, such as having more love, peace, adventure, freedom, achievement, balance, or success. Once your clients articulate what they want as a coaching outcome, you will explore why this outcome is important to them, especially now. To feel satisfied and happy, what they want will be in alignment with a life value now or in a defined future.

Here is a list of common life values:

Achievement: Successful completion of visible tasks and projects

Advancement: Getting ahead, aspiring to higher levels

Adventure: Challenge, risk-taking, testing limits

Aesthetics: Desire for beautiful surroundings, artistic expression

Challenge: Testing physical or mental limits

Community: Neighbors or coworkers who are familiar, friendly, and helpful

Competence: Being good at what you do, capable, effective

Creativity: Finding new ways to do things, composing, discovering

Environment: Respecting the earth and living in safe, comfortable spaces

Fairness: Respecting everyone's rights

Family: Taking care of and spending time with relatives

Freedom: Ability to make one's own decisions and choices

Friendship: Close companionship, ongoing and supportive relationships

Health: Maintaining and enhancing physical well-being

Helping: Taking care of others, assisting others to flourish

Honesty: Being sincere and truthful, keeping promises

Humor: Fun, lightness, spontaneity

Independence: Self-reliance, autonomy

Inner harmony: Freedom from inner conflict, feeling integrated or whole

Integrity: Acting in line with beliefs, doing what you said you would

Intellect: Learning about and discussing an area of knowledge

Intimacy: Deep connection with others

Peace: Harmony among people and groups

Perseverance: Pushing through to the end, completing tasks and goals

Personal growth: Continual learning and personal development

Pleasure: Personal satisfaction, enjoyment, delight

Position: Being highly regarded in one's social group

Power: Having the authority or ability to direct events or
make things happen

Prosperity: Flourishing, being well-off, easily obtaining
desires

Religion: Deep connection with one's faith

Security: Freedom from worry, safety from threats

Spirituality: Belief in the divine and an unseen nonhuman
power

Stability: Certainty, predictability

Teamwork: Cooperating with others toward a common goal

Tradition: Respecting the way things have been done in
the past

Winning: Success when competing, coming out on top

The downside of values is their rigidity. If you believe others
should have values similar to yours, you might not be able to
connect and collaborate with those who have different values,
whether at work or at home. I often find in coaching that when
clients can't accept other people's or an organization's values,
they hold on tightly to what they believe is right and resist seeing another way forward. They won't compromise. They only
want to convince others their values are wrong. All I can do as
their coach is to reflect their stance. They have to decide what
to do with the impasse.

Share what you notice about their behavior and explore the
impact on their work, their relationships, their health, and their
desires. They may shift or choose to do something else in time—
or not.

A. H. Almaas says in his book *The Unfolding Now,* "As we become
more and more attuned to what is happening in our experience,
our capacity to understand ourselves at increasingly subtler levels

continues to develop."[8] Your clients learn about themselves and expand their frames when exploring beliefs, emotional expressions, unmet needs, and values conflicts. This process can happen many times in a person's life as the meanings of significant events unfold.

Three Tips for Brain Hacking by Coaching What Holds Together Your Clients' Stories

Clients will give you everything you need to coach them. Their thoughts have been circulating in their heads. When you obstruct this thinking process with reflective inquiry, the obstruction causes them to pause, step back, and explore their thinking—the beliefs, fears, incongruities in values and desires, and needs related to their dilemma. They see their stories in a new way. This brain hacking provides the new perspective clients need to formulate a different view of their situations and see new ways to move forward. Here are some tips to help you disrupt your clients' thinking so they are willing and able to use a new perspective to achieve their desired outcomes.

1. *Resist judging the beliefs shaping clients' stories.* Be open to your clients' interpretations of their dilemmas. Let them tell the full story, at least until they start repeating themselves. Listen for words they emphasize and key words such as *really*, *but*, and *should*. Actively replay what you hear and notice to help them pare their story down to the essential elements. Start your sentences with phrases such as "So I heard you say you think the reason this is happening is . . ." or "You got very angry (excited, quiet, defensive, etc.) when you described . . ." Make sure your tone is encouraging and inquisitive. Keep your opinions, judgments, and analysis out of the conversation. Releasing

judgment builds the trust necessary for clients to jump in and explore with you.

2. *Notice their emotional reactions and shifts.* They will get angry or sad when explaining what they hoped would transpire. Listen for statements such as "They promised me . . . ," "I can't work under these circumstances," "It's happening again," or even "That's it. I'm done." Encourage your clients to discuss what they hoped would happen but didn't. What made the situation uncomfortable or awful? Once the unmet need is identified, clients can then choose to work on getting their needs met or on letting them go. They might decide to live with an unmet need for now if it leads to a better future.

3. *Affirm clients' efforts and intentions, especially if these relate to their life values.* You encourage disclosure when you sincerely share, "I know you are trying to be the best leader you can be," "You worked hard to give your children opportunities," or "I can tell you are committed to getting the best results on this project." This allows you to explore what needs to be resolved to be in alignment with clients' values and which consequences would be difficult to live with. If clients indicate they have tried all the options they know of and are willing to take, you can ask, "If you have done your best with what you know, what is in your control to do now?" When clients confidently make choices on their own, they no longer feel stuck.

CHAPTER 6

GOALTENDING

Staying the Course

*One's destination is never a place but
rather a new way of looking at things.*

—Henry Miller

NO MATTER WHAT you are exploring when coaching, you must be clear about where the conversation is going throughout the session. Without a clear, desired outcome for the conversation, clients can have revelations when talking through a dilemma, but they might not apply their insights to achieving what they really want. The difficult part of keeping the conversation on track is that what clients state they want to achieve at the start of the session will expand, shift, or completely change as you explore their beliefs, needs, values, and doubts. The new destination for the coaching must then be agreed on to ensure movement toward it by the end of the session. The moment clients commit to what they will do next to get what they *really* want, they feel a sense of completion.

THE BOOKENDS OF COACHING

When you stand up a row of books, you need strong objects on both ends to keep the books upright. These placeholders also mark the beginning and end of the row. You can swap, add, or remove books easily between the bookends. You can even change what you use as bookends, but you can't remove either bookend without the row falling apart.

> Establishing the bookends of coaching—the desired outcome and the commitment to the next step—is vital to ensure clients see through their frames and then do something new.

With no desired outcome, client stories ramble and often run in circles. While talking, clients might give new meaning to a piece of their story. They might even feel better about their role in the story, but the relief and confidence clients feel after talking out their problems is short-lived. They go back to their busy, complex lives and are quickly consumed by the overwhelm, anger, or powerlessness they felt at the start of the coaching session. Their story will continue to be a frustrating dilemma.

> Clarifying the desired outcome gives the coach guardrails to keep the story from falling off the edge of a forward-moving path.

Three important practices for coaches to create strong book-ends are (1) unwrapping what clients want instead of what they have now ("What do you want?"), (2) tracking their progress toward the stated outcome and tracking changes in the outcome for clients to confirm or restate ("What do you *really* want?"), and (3) coaching clients to crystalize their insights and commit to actions they will take to ensure progress toward their desired outcome ("What will you do now?") (fig. 5).

This chapter will help you clarify and unwrap the best outcome for a client to move toward in the conversation. With a clear outcome in place, the coaching can then focus on what is getting in the way of this smart, resourceful client from achieving his or her desired outcome. Then you will learn how to track the coaching session so you stay focused on a desired result as it transforms. You will learn how to wrap up your session to ensure a commitment to growth in chapter 7.

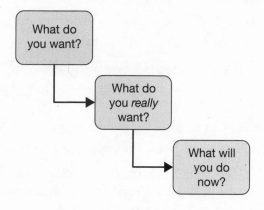

Figure 5. The path of coaching.

UNWRAPPING THE DESIRED OUTCOME

A coaching session can be compared to the creative process of freestyle rap. Neuroscientists at the National Institute on Deafness and Other Communication Disorders scanned the brains of twelve professional rappers with an fMRI (functional magnetic resonance imaging) machine. The scientists discovered that although the brain's executive functions were active at the start and end of a song, during freestyle, the parts of the brain responsible for self-monitoring, critiquing, and editing were deactivated. In this context, the researchers explained that the rappers were "freed from the conventional constraints of supervisory attention and executive control," so sudden insights could easily emerge.[1]

In other words, the rappers used the executive functions of their cognitive brains as they started rapping to deliberately set the intention of the composition up front. Once they had a sense of where they were going, they switched off their inner critic and analyzer. This allowed for more activity in the inner brain, where the eruption of new ideas—creativity—takes place. As they moved to closing out the song, their cognitive brains came back online to provide a consciously designed ending to the composition.

Like a rap, most of coaching should be spontaneous interactions with clients to surface beliefs, needs, values, and fears getting in the way of achieving a specific outcome. When the coach and client know the desired destination of the coaching session, the coach can more easily work in the present without much thought to identify what is keeping the client stuck. The interaction flows freely until they move to wrap it up at the end.

Although envisioning what the client truly wants might sound easy, it's not. Stories trigger an emotional fog, clouding the view. Clients say, "I don't know what I want" or "That's what I need to do, to figure out what I want." Don't push them to see into the future. Relax and listen to their story. With reflection and curiosity, the emotional fog will dissipate. The outcome might not become clear in one session, but clients begin to understand better what they need to know to feel content with the direction they choose to take.

An Outcome Is Not a Problem or Process

It's okay to start a session by asking, "What would you like to talk about today?" But don't leave it there. Clients often jump in with the story that is circulating in their minds, generally one that is emotionally taxing. Fixing the problem in the story is not an outcome. To clarify what could get better or be achieved as a result of your time together, listen for key words and emotional shifts as clients talk. Share what you are noticing and ask how they would like this story to end. If the story represents a reoccurring pattern of behavior for your clients or the other people in the story, ask what they would like to have happen differently the next time this predicament arises.

The outcome often takes time to emerge. Once they envision an outcome they truly want, not one that others want for them, clients are more willing to commit to at least one step that will move them forward.

Case Study

The client was a senior vice president of human resources for a major retail chain. She said she felt completely overwhelmed and didn't know where to start. She asked me to help her with prioritizing her tasks. My response was "For the past three years, you have excelled at your job. Before that, you were a successful attorney who graduated from Stanford. Based on your achievements, I bet you discovered how to prioritize years ago. So I'm curious: do you want to figure out *how* to prioritize or see if we can figure out what's making it so hard for you to prioritize now?"

After a long pause, she said she feared she was losing her motivation. She wasn't sure why she was fighting her daily battles. She had lost a sense of what could be next for her career.

I said, "I hear two desires. Do you want to clarify the value, maybe the purpose, of your current job, or do you want to explore the possibilities you have for your future?"

"Wow," she said. "You just reminded me that I had a purpose and a vision when I took this job three years ago. My husband and I had a dream of owning a business together. We've both gotten so busy, I have no idea if he still wants to do this. Maybe that's why I can't see my future, especially through the messes I face today. I need to talk to him about this." We agreed to reschedule the session in three days after she had a chance to speak with her husband.

When we reconvened, she said, "Our dream is alive. You were right. I don't need your help prioritizing. I figure I need to be here a few more years to solidify the knowledge and experience I need to step into our dream successfully. With that, I would like some coaching on how to reset my relationship with the CEO." We started by envisioning what a desirable, and achievable, relationship looked like.

Typically, clients recognize the best solution to their dilemma as soon as they declare what they really want. Articulating their desired outcome may take a few minutes or half an hour as you sort through their stories. Then, even if they determine what they need to do now, they may need to muster courage and gain additional support to take the first step. Clarifying the outcome helps clients either see a new way forward or face what they knew they had to do all along. They can't see this for themselves, especially when they are consumed by stress.

Most sessions start with identifying a problem to solve. Sometimes clients think they can resolve the dilemma if they sort through options and make a decision or they complete a list or plan to know what to do next. None of these actions define the outcome. You want to determine what solving the problem, making the decision, or completing the list or plan will give them. If they say the process they are requesting will help them know what step they need to take, you can start by sorting through options or items to put in their lists or plans. Then, during the session, you may discover a clearer picture of what vision they want to move toward. When you explore what is driving their urge to solve the problem or make the decision or plan now, you will unearth desires—possibly fears. If you ask what they would do if they were brave or what would they regret not doing a year from now, they might be able to fill in some details of the outcome they really want.

Clients often come to the conversation with a goal to make a decision, but the real problem is that they have made a decision they are afraid to step into. This is a common scenario when someone wants to leave a job, turn down a project, or take an action that could hurt a relationship. Their fears are compounded by guilt. When they explain their options, their emotions will likely reveal their preference despite their fears. Admitting to their preference will help them identify what is causing their fear and guilt and if the consequences are real, assumed, or exaggerated. The outcome they want to achieve is not making a decision; it is the vision of living their preference. Coaching then helps them determine when and how to take action considering which consequences they determined were real.

Another example is when clients claim they want more balance when they are really feeling unfulfilled, unappreciated, or under pressure to perform at work or at home. If you accept their initial goal of balance as the outcome, you will focus on time or task management. Instead, if you dig deeper to find out what is really draining their energy, not only will the flow of the conversation be more meaningful but knowing there is hope for the future will make their present circumstances more palatable.

People are often unsure what they want, or they are afraid to speak it out loud. Your job is to help them name what they want. Once their real desires are articulated, the actions they must take are easier to declare and commit to.

Case Study

The client said her goal was to work with two of the leaders on her project team to create a solid action plan everyone would agree to. After sorting through activities she would like to see in the plan, I said, "You seem to have solid options to present to these two leaders. What do you want them to do with your suggestions once you present them?"

"I just want them to get their act together and agree to something. Those two guys are on opposite ends of the spectrum on what we need to do, but neither of them is budging. Time is running out. Jobs are on the line. How do I make them see that?"

Her agitation was palpable. I asked, "How responsible are you for the outcome of the project?"

"My job could be on the line too, but they don't report to me, so I can't make them do anything. What if they ignore me?"

"I see how frustrated you are with their conflict in light of the urgency of having a plan. Are you afraid nothing will happen regardless of what you offer?"

"Yes, but since I'm not their boss, I can't really draw a line, can I?"

"I don't know, can you? What's the worst that can happen if you do?"

"They ignore me, which won't change anything we have now."

"What will happen if you don't?"

"I have to make something happen now or all our jobs are on the line."

"So I hear your goal is to confront this situation head-on by drawing the line, by which I think you mean stating the bottom line of what needs to happen now and why. Right?"

"Yes. I just need to say it. What needs to happen now and why. Out loud, firmly so they hear me." Her resolve was much stronger than when we started. The conversation moved toward achieving the newly defined outcome of confidently stating the bottom line and getting the leaders' commitment to at least negotiate a plan. Then she could present her suggestions.

Once you listen to a client's story and how he defines the problem, listen for the following:

+ *What does the person want to happen, even if he is uncomfortable saying it?* Summarize, paraphrase, and encapsulate what the person perceives. Ask what he wants to have happen that he is not getting now. If he keeps slipping back into detailing the problem, bottom line the outcome you think he desires to achieve based on the story he is telling and ask for confirmation. Accept his response.

+ *What does the person feel is most important?* Listen for a shift in emotion that indicates unmet needs. The client might even say, "What I *really* want . . ." or "Why can't they just do this . . ."

+ *What is causing the person's frustration, guilt, fear, or embarrassment?* When a client uses the word *but*, explore the reality of the consequence he names after the *but*. The words following *but* generally describe a person's fears or a limiting perception of what he must tolerate. Exploring this dynamic could lead the person to identifying a fulfilling outcome, even if achieving it will cause discomfort.

When you share what you heard and the emotions you noticed, you can better explore the client's difficulty in stating what he wants instead of what he has. Then you can coach him to realize how he wants the story to end.

Topic versus Outcome

Clients might have only a topic to discuss, such as how to improve their leadership presence, how to deal with their reluctance to change, or how to build relationships with peers. Coaching doesn't have to be about problem-solving. You may focus on personal or professional development.

You can still coach clients toward at least a preliminary outcome of the conversation, asking questions such as "What will you find easier to do once we explore this topic?" or "What is prompting you to talk about this now?" or "How will you know you are improving if you work on this?" Guide them to describe one scenario they would like to improve or define as a measure of success so coaching leads to progress in their development.

If clients are reluctant to designate an outcome, let them describe where they feel they are today in relation to their topic so you can pull out what sounds like a direction they would like to take, such as to have a more fulfilling job, to take better care of themselves, or to act with more confidence. Then you can invite them to describe what *better* or *more* might look like to start getting a sense of a destination.

Case Study

In a session I observed, the client said she wanted to talk about how people know they are choosing to do what they are passionate about. The coach asked what prompted her to want to talk about passion. The client said her pattern was to work on achieving her dream, but as soon as she feared she would fail, she changed course. She gave examples of studying dance and then shifting to stage production when she lost confidence in her ability to succeed on the stage. Then she studied journalism but shifted to website design when she questioned her writing skills. Now she was interested in learning interior design to partner with her husband, who owned a home remodeling business. When the coach asked if she felt passionate about interior design, the client responded, "I am not sure being a designer is my passion, though I'm enjoying learning about it. But how will I ever know if I have a passion for something if I don't stick with it?"

The coach then asked, "Would you like to focus on how you will know if you are passionate about a choice you have made, or do you want to explore how to strengthen your confidence to

---

stick with your goal?" The client chose to explore how she could confidently persist when her fears showed up. The coach continued the inquiry by asking her what she would gain by sticking with one career. The client then described what it might feel like to succeed at one thing and why that was important to her. The coaching proceeded with this destination in mind.

Sometimes you can ask clients to visualize the best-case scenario related to the topic. You might ask questions such as "What does a strong leadership presence look like to you?" or "When other people embrace change, what do they do differently than you?" or "If you had great relationships at work, what would they look like?" The outcome will probably evolve once you coach them on what they need to do to move forward, but it's good to start with a visible destination.

> Articulating the outcome is the conduit
> between uncertainty and progress.

Clients often remain confused and discouraged and coaches feel they are letting their clients down if an achievable destination isn't defined. Clarifying the outcome is one of the most powerful acts of coaching.

TRACKING PROGRESS AND ALTERATIONS IN THE OUTCOME

The process of drilling down to discover what a person really wants to resolve or achieve is often referred to as *peeling the onion*. A shift in the picture or a new outcome is revealed as you pare off layers of old beliefs and chip away at the armor protecting vulnerabilities. Then, either the visual of the outcome changes or it expands with a focus on new details.

Whether the outcome subtly shifts or it completely changes, you need to notice the shifts and changes and then make sure the client is okay with altering the direction of the conversation. Your client may choose to go back to the original outcome. Your job is to ensure the conversation is moving in a desired direction throughout the conversation so you don't chase your client down distracting side roads.

The movement of a *shift* in desired outcome can be in one of the following aspects:

+ The orientation of the outcome (shifting from solving the external problem to clarifying the personal dilemma to be resolved)

+ One's relationship to the outcome (keeping the outcome the same but envisioning oneself differently when defining what success looks like when the outcome is achieved)

+ The pacing of achievement of the outcome (choosing to make a change immediately or moving the destination into the future with a longer range plan)

A client might choose to completely *change* the outcome. I often see this occur when clients say they want to find a way to change an undesirable situation at home or work. Then, when exploring their frustration, they blurt out their real desire to do something else. They have lost their drive to make things better. They have already decided to change but haven't taken the steps to initiate the process. The coach, after reflecting the declaration and emotions expressed, still invites the client to choose the outcome to work on *now*. The client can opt to look at a different vision or stick with the initial outcome that was defined for now.

Horizontal versus Vertical Coaching to Define the Outcome

Horizontal coaching occurs when you use the initial client outcome as the destination for the session. You may ask a question to explore the meaning of words used in the client's description or inquire about the importance of the outcome. Once the client responds, you might ask a few follow-up questions (fig. 6).

The objective of horizontal coaching is to formulate plans to move forward. The plans are often generic. Clients could probably create these plans without a coach if they took time to think about what they wanted to create. They use the coaching to sort through ideas, which is useful, but reasons that made the planning difficult to do on their own will likely reappear in the future.

Vertical coaching expands awareness. Outcomes tend to evolve as the coaching reveals desires for more personal goals or courageous commitments. Shifts are made at the identity level instead of just looking for new ways to solve a problem. In other words, you coach the person, not the problem.

Although vertical coaching also starts with what clients say they want from the coaching sessions and why this is important to them, it quickly moves to reflecting the beliefs you hear clients state when describing the dilemma that is hindering achievement of the desired outcome (fig. 7). Exploring beliefs might lead to identifying fears that social needs won't be met or possible

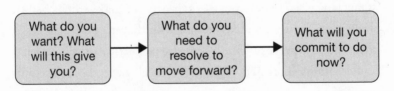

Figure 6. Horizontal coaching.

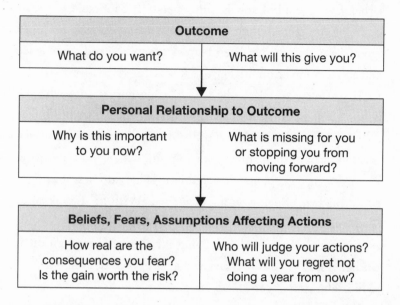

Figure 7. Vertical coaching—examples of questions.

conflicts in values. In the process of this exploration, either the beliefs or the outcome shifts or changes.

Sometimes clients just need a safe place to talk through options horizontally, but if they struggle making a decision or finding solutions, awareness-based vertical coaching is more effective than solution-focused horizontal coaching to resolve what is getting in the way of what they want to create.

For example, if you coach leaders, you will inevitably have a session focused on how the leader will approach a difficult conversation. You may ask what a successful conversation would look like. The leader will describe a positive interchange. Horizontal coaching would look at what might happen to derail the outcome and then what the leader will do to handle these disturbances. I've had these conversations. The leader may still delay the conversation. Or the leader may report an unsatisfactory result where he either gave in, not holding the other person accountable, or ended up being directive, telling the person what to do with no other interaction. The leader often blames organizational precedence and expectations from higher-ups for having to be directive.

If you were to coach the leader to go deeper into what he believes will make the conflict difficult, he might describe his fear of handling emotions that could show up. The outcome of the coaching would then shift to staying calm when emotions arise. Then, when you explore what could rattle his calmness, he might reveal his fear of being wrong or judged. With further exploration, you land on a belief such as "Just having to have this difficult conversation means I failed at being a leader." The recognition of the belief leads to a conversation that shifts the desired outcome to his definition of good leadership.

When talking about leadership, Brené Brown says most people have been taught to believe that vulnerability is a weakness. "It's hard, and it's awkward. And, we don't want to do it because we feel if we put ourselves out there, we're going to get hurt. We're going to fail. We're going to be a disappointment."[2] Vertical coaching is needed for leaders, or anyone, to disclose why they are avoiding a difficult conversation. You might ask, "What would you do if you were brave?" The outcome will probably shift again.

What's Getting in the Way?

My colleague and brilliant leadership coach in Singapore, Tony Latimer, says his coaching model is to find out what clients want and then coach them to discover what is getting in the way of their getting what they want. They often can't see or won't admit to what's getting in the way. Once the block to progress is revealed, clients can better choose what they want to do next.

I add a few layers to Tony's model to include the evolving outcome. Each time the outcome shifts, there is a new exploration around, "What's getting in the way?" (fig. 8).

Exploring what is getting in the way of the smart, creative people you are coaching means you are curious about the beliefs, social needs, and values that hold their story together. Start with reflecting the beliefs you hear that define their story and the emotional shifts you notice. Then you can move into the context to see what they fear they will lose or not get if they don't commit to act now.

Your reflections and questions might uncover the social needs at play. For example, a leader might share her fear of losing respect or credibility for a decision she has made. You might even uncover a conflict of values, where the leader feels the easy solution to the

Figure 8. Discovering the real desired outcome.

problem impacts her integrity ("It's not who I am"). Yet she fears if she does what she really wants to do, she will be judged as being weak or not supportive of the bigger picture.

Case Study

A client hired me to help her earn a promotion in her all-male engineering department. She excelled at her work, and she established good one-on-one relationships with her peers.

Her greatest challenge was changing her behaviors in team meetings. She described that when discussing solutions to problems, she hesitated and then impatiently blurted out what was wrong with people's ideas before saying what she would do. She knew she wanted to ask more questions before offering her ideas for consideration, so her initial outcome was clear.

In the next coaching session, she said she was unsuccessful in changing her behavior. We went deeper into what beliefs were getting in her way. She said, "I want to make sure the ideas I put forth make sense. But then people get to arguing and talking over each other so much, I get frustrated finding the right moment to break in. So I barge in. I can tell they judge me as a pushy woman. Then I scream at them and they judge me as a bitchy woman." I asked how she knew her peers were seeing her that way. She said she never asked them what they thought. She said that since she had good relationships with them outside the meeting, she could ask them individually.

I asked her to describe how she wanted to show up in meetings, not just thinking about the words she wanted to say but visualizing her presence. After pausing to think, she said, "I want to be an inspirational leader, not just an idea generator." I asked if that was the outcome she wanted to work to create. With her

---

agreement, we looked more deeply at what was causing her hesitation and then anger in the meetings. She ended by saying she wanted to find a more powerful, not pushy, way to ask for the floor when she had an idea. Then, when she had people's attention, she would draw a picture of what they could accomplish together with her idea. She wanted to address how they could take risks and support each other to grow. I acknowledged her for stepping into her leadership shoes and then asked her to create a best-case scenario. From there, she listed the steps she would take in her next meeting.

Some clients might not believe they can achieve their desired outcome. I worked with a client who wanted to prepare for a difficult conversation with a woman who reported to him. As he started to plan, he said, "It won't work. She won't change."

I asked, "If this is true, what do you need to do?"

He said he thought he could find some way to fix the situation, but he really wanted to help her find a new job she might enjoy better. The conversation would still be difficult, but his outcome shifted.

Once an outcome is stated, check the beliefs around what is achievable now. Clients may admit to unreasonable expectations, which will alter their outcome. If they don't know if their desire is achievable, they may commit to researching what it will take to realistically achieve what they want. What *researching* looks like becomes the outcome.

Keeping the Outcome in Mind Even as It Shifts

While coaching, you want to keep in mind, "Where are we going?" If the outcome was clarified but the conversation is going deeper, ask if the outcome is still valid. As the client's perspective shifts, ask what is becoming clearer or what the client now understands. Then share if you notice the conversation is going in a new direction. Let the client choose to refine the focus or shift the view of the outcome.

Case Study

The client started by saying one of his peers made fun of a gay employee in a leadership team meeting made up of all-male director-level peers and three vice presidents. The client said, "I spoke up, saying that with all the diversity issues, the conversation was not okay." He said one of the VPs agreed. They went back to the meeting agenda. After the meeting, the VP suggested they meet later that week for lunch. The client wanted to use the coaching session to talk about the upcoming lunch meeting.

The coach asked, "What do you want to come away with from your meeting?"

"I don't want it to be about diversity. But maybe it should be. Is it my leadership responsibility to bring this up? I don't think anyone knows I'm gay, but why should that matter? Shouldn't they care about diversity too? What I really want to talk about with the VP is my leadership potential in the company. I want to know what he sees for me and maybe what I need to develop."

"You seem to have two areas to focus on in the conversation. Taking a role in the company's drive for diversity and exploring your leadership opportunities."

The client said that unless the VP brings up diversity, he didn't want to create a divide with his peers by being seen as the "diversity police." Even if the topic did come up in conversation, he wanted to talk with the VP about his leadership overall. He wanted to build a good relationship.

With questions from the coach, the client clarified what he wanted out of the conversation with the VP. But then the session cycled back to the diversity conversation and how it made him uncomfortable. The coach asked if the client wanted to shift the focus of the coaching to see what he would need to feel comfortable talking about diversity. The client said he would like to look at being comfortable with being an advocate, but first he wanted to make sure he could be an advocate without being seen as a fanatic. So the coaching outcome changed to how the client could successfully advocate for diversity without being seen as a fanatic.

After exploring the distinction between advocate and fanatic, the coach asked what this meant to the client in terms of his behavior at work. The client said that he now felt comfortable with how he would address his role in the company's push for diversity, so he wanted to go back to talking about his conversation with the VP. The coach confirmed they were shifting the outcome back to what a successful conversation with the VP would be for him.

While exploring his fears, the client began talking about his view of what it takes to be a great leader. He said he wanted to show up courageously with honesty, even when talking about difficult issues like diversity and inclusion. He said he knew he could be a target of ridicule, but he now realized acting with integrity was more important than impressing the VP.

The coach then asked if envisioning the leader he wanted to be was the most important outcome for the client. The client said, "Yes, I want to be *that* leader in every conversation. It's not about advocacy; it's about leadership." The coach acknowledged the client's new awareness and resolve. They spent the remaining time refining the client's definition of leadership, what it looked like, and what it would take for him to become this kind of leader in whatever company he worked for.

Inviting and Reinviting

Sometimes clients are so emotionally attached to their stories, they just keep restating the problem multiple ways instead of defining what they want. Even if they start to envision what an outcome might look like, they run back to describing past difficulties.

To avoid going backward in a session, firmly state that no progress will be made if they can't find one positive outcome to move toward. You may need to ask multiple times what outcome they would like to create. Or you can choose one of their problems and invite them to describe a scene where the outcome is solved. If they are game, you then ask, "Is this the outcome you want to explore in our coaching, or is something more pressing for you?" Again, you may need to make this invitation numerous times.

Case Study

The client was looking to find a new job after not working for a year due to health issues. She said she had the green light from her doctor to get a full-time job and she wanted to use the coaching to create a self-care plan.

Once it became clear she already had a plan, the coach asked if she wanted to look at how to best implement her plan when she started a new job. She said yes but also acknowledged her typical pattern was to start out strong until her fears of inadequacy led her to overwork. Then she increased her stress by getting mad at herself. The coach asked if the client wanted to stay with the outcome of sticking with her self-care plan or look at building her confidence on the job so she didn't feel she needed to overwork. The client chose to work on building her confidence, saying she wanted to feel "tall and strong" at work.

As she explored her feelings of inadequacy, the client dropped back into describing her history of illness and injuries. The coach reaffirmed with the client that she felt healthy enough to work now and then asked if she wanted to look at being "tall and strong" in terms of confidence or health. The client said that when she loses her confidence, she overworks and hurts her health, which in turn drags down her confidence even more. She wanted to stick to looking at how to build her confidence. But as the client talked about her fears of inadequacy, she fell back into talking about her physical capacity.

The coach asked, "How real is the possibility that you will not have the physical stamina for the job?"

The client said, "I don't know, I'm just worried."

The coach said, "You said that so resolutely. Is that the real dilemma here, that you are just worried?"

The client laughed. "Yes, I create a storm in my head. I'm doing this to me."

"So your vision is still to be tall and strong at work?"

"Yes, I believe I can be."

"You have moved from adhering to a self-care plan to building and sustaining your confidence, but you now see that your success hinges on the effects of your worry. Is this true?"

"Yes, I make it up until it's real. I make myself sick with worry."

"What a great insight. What do you want to do with your worry?"

From here, with the same outcome of being tall and strong at work, the session shifted to addressing her habit of worry. In the end, the client said she felt content with her plan to find a job where she could ease back into the workforce with confidence and care.

Coaching is supportive and encouraging; it can also be uncomfortable and disconcerting when you have to steer the client to stay in the present moment with a view of the future. Once, after a coaching demonstration, someone in the audience asked the client if I annoyed her with how I kept redirecting her to an outcome in the coaching. She replied, "Yes, it was very annoying. And it was exactly what I needed." You aren't coaching to make clients feel better. You are there to help them see better—with clarity and confidence.

Three Tips for Keeping the Conversation on Track

A coaching session needs to have a destination to keep it from being just a conversation about a problem. Even though clients may sort through their thinking while they talk, if the coach helps them clearly identify what they want to create to replace what they now have, the resolutions will be more profound and lasting. Because problems can have many layers, outcomes often morph and change during the session. Use the following tips to enhance your goaltending while coaching:

1. *When clients list a number of problems, encapsulate what you hear and invite them to choose what outcome they want to work toward first.* Use their words to frame the invitation. An example is "Do you want your boss to treat you differently, or do you want to redefine your job so you wake up more excited to go to work?" Paring down options to work on one outcome gives clients both a clear destination and an affirmation of their greatest desire. If clients are reluctant to designate an outcome, let them describe where they feel they are today in relation to their topic. Then invite them to paint a vision that expresses what a better picture might look like.

2. *Recognize when the outcome shifts and reflect this to the client, using the client's words.* As clients examine their beliefs, assumptions, fears, and deeper desires, you may hear a shift in what they want as an end result. The shift could be big if the coaching moves from solving an external problem to resolving an internal dilemma that is exacerbating the problem. Or the shift might be a small change in direction or priorities after the client has a clearer view of the situation. Share what you are noticing about the shift in focus and ask how this relates to the original outcome. If the client agrees that what he wants is taking on a new form, ask him to restate the new outcome to ensure you both agree on the picture and the meaning.

3. *Listen for repeated words and emotional trigger points that spark anger, excuses, or blame.* Share what you hear and notice. Repeated words such as *control*, *not listening*, and *it's too much* are clues to defining what the client really wants. Ask how these words relate to the stated outcome. You might hear what the client fears she will lose or not get if she doesn't resolve the problem, such as respect, credibility, security, or being liked. Does she need to change the picture to include getting her needs met? You might uncover a conflict of values, where the client feels what she wants isn't what others think she *should* want—if she does what she really wants to do, she will fail or hurt others. As the client's perspective shifts with new realizations, ask what is becoming clearer or what she now understands. Then ask if she would like to refine the outcome based on her new awareness. Imagining, refining, and redefining outcomes helps keep conversations moving forward instead of going in circles.

CHAPTER 7

NEW AND NEXT

Coaching Insights and Commitments

Until one is committed, there is hesitancy,
the chance to draw back, always ineffectiveness.

—William H. Murray

A COMMON REGRET of coaches occurs when they realize they missed the opportunity to confirm clients will define and commit to an action, even if the action is to take time to reflect. The opportunity missed does not happen after clients make a decision. The oversight comes when coaches don't ask about a slight smile, gasp, or look of shock that indicates clients have landed on a truth or solution they had not seen before.

Here's the scenario: The client had a powerful new awareness about himself or his situation. The coach felt good about the shift in perspective—so good, the coach forgot to make sure the shift in perspective is clear and then leverage the new awareness into a commitment to act.

This lapse is common because of the strong emotional shifts accompanying insight formation. As the new meaning comes into view, the client may experience embarrassment, sadness, or unease. If the coach holds a safe space for the client to process his reaction, he generally moves into acceptance. The discomfort subsides. He often breathes a sigh of relief. Coach and client share a sense of liberation; the client is finally free to move on.

The release feels like the end of the journey; it is not. It's like when your bid to buy a house is accepted. You celebrate. Then you face the many steps you have to take to make the house your home.

> When clients experience a new insight, they feel as if a door has opened to a new way of seeing. They have yet to walk through the door.

Coaches may remember to ask if clients know what they want to do now that they see their situation differently. That's not enough. Clients might say, "I know exactly what to do now, thank you." They feel a sense of completion. Coaches may ask if clients have anything more to discuss, and clients will happily say no.

Without formally wrapping up the coaching session with a verbalized commitment to action, clients may forget what they thought they knew to do after the session ends. They might even lose the insight they had. They can remember they gained clarity on what needs to be resolved. They might have even articulated a few steps to take, but without exploring what could get in the way of implementing their plan, a host of circumstances could hinder their progress.

In chapter 6, you read about the need to provide bookends for your coaching, starting with defining the outcome of the coaching session. The row of books must be held up on both ends to keep the books upright. The bookend at the end of the row—the commitment to the next step—ensures clients crystalize their insights and the actions they will take to move toward their desired outcome.

YOU HAVE TO SAY IT OUT LOUD TO MAKE IT REAL

Before clients move into action, it's important to anchor the new perspective by asking them to articulate what they are now seeing or learning. Then you can get their commitment to apply what they have learned before the conversation is over.

Much of coaching is shepherding clients to see what they have resisted or overlooked. Telling you their story is like recapping the scene of a play. They don't notice all the details of the scene. They see only the props and actors in a way that supports the meaning they assigned to the narrative.

The brain is a meaning-making machine. It pulls from past experiences, old beliefs, ongoing fears, and present assumptions to instantly define what the senses take in. Coaching is intended to examine the meaning people give to situations to determine what else could be going on that would change their approach going forward. Imagine you are walking down the street. You notice a brown object on the sidewalk in front of you. You instantly determine it's a rock. As you get closer, you notice the rock is really a paper bag. When you reach the bag, a squirrel dashes out. You gasp and laugh at the realization.

When your coaching brings what was overlooked or avoided to the surface, the sudden clarity can be surprising and often humbling. When what was concealed is revealed, the epiphany will trigger an emotional reaction in your clients. The reaction could be light with laughter or heavy with silence and full of guilt. The emotion could bring tears or an angry outburst. Clients might abruptly avert their gaze. Their eyes might glaze over and they might stop breathing.

No matter the intensity of the shift, don't sympathize or try to diminish the feeling. They will breathe again. Use silence to allow them to fully experience the moment. Monitor your own breathing and patiently sit with the silence for about double the time you would normally tolerate.

Although you will give clients space to process their reactions, you don't want to let this powerful moment slip by. They may start speaking on their own. No matter where they go in the conversation, or if they continue to be quiet, be sure to ask them, "Would you share with me what just happened? What are you seeing now?" The articulation may be immediate. They might need to talk through what they are coming to understand. Verbally processing the details can help the new belief take shape. As botanist Robin Wall Kimmerer said, "Finding the words is another step in learning to see." Give clients all the space they need to understand what has emerged.

Giving words to what has been revealed is like seeing where a jigsaw puzzle piece fits in the picture. Articulating the learning and insights locks the piece into place in the story. The client and coach have a shared understanding to work with.

The client said she wanted to clarify what her business would look like if she had the courage to do only what inspired her. She said her fear of failure was keeping her small. The coach took a number of paths with her. First, he asked her to describe what "being small" looked like. Then, he asked her to name what she was yearning to do so they could identify an outcome to work toward. Then, the coach asked the client what was wasting her time. The client willingly responded to the inquiries but kept her arms close to her body the entire time.

The coach said, "This isn't the first time you've had this conversation. You know what playing bigger looks and feels like to you. You know where you are today, so you can define the gap. I want to know, what are you holding in?"

With some irritation, the client declared, "I just don't want to work that hard!"

The coach said, "Got it."

The client sat back in her chair. Her entire body relaxed.

The coach said, "Should we start all over?"

"I'm not sure I can create a new picture of my future," the client said. "I've been talking about playing a bigger game for a long time."

"Let's start with your saying out loud what you finally allowed yourself to see, okay? Would you tell me what just became clear for you?"

After a moment of thought, the client said, "I want to make changes to what I do, I know I can do more than what I'm doing now, but I don't want my work to consume my life."

The coach then asked the client to lay out what she most enjoyed about her work now so she could begin to piece together a vision that felt right for her to work toward creating.

The shift that accompanies a new awareness could be slight, like when clients willingly accept fallacies in the assumptions in their story, or more profound, which often happens when clients explore the weight of social needs and values. The awareness might change their frame. These breakthroughs occur when the result of the insight strengthens or expands their perception of self in relation to a dilemma (identity) or they discover an entirely new view of what they now believe is true (reality). All these realizations must be articulated to crystallize the change in the frame.

Notice when the insight indicates a possible new outcome to achieve in the coaching. Statements such as "I don't want to work so hard" or "I've been avoiding the risk" or "It's hard for me to give up what I thought was the right way to be" or even "What a jerk I've been" could point to a new desired outcome. Invite clients to choose the direction of the coaching. Are they ready to look at what actions to take now, or do they want to redefine what they want to achieve based on the insight they shared? If they say they are clear about what they want to do now, ask how their actions will help them achieve the outcome they agreed to earlier in the session. If they say they want to make a plan but they will need to resolve something else, ask if they would like to address this new complication now or in the next session. The choice of what outcome to work toward always belongs to the client.

WHAT NOW?

So how do you know when to move into closing out the conversation with a commitment to action? It might be when clients land on an acceptable resolution to what was keeping them from achieving their desired outcome. It could be the moment they discover what they *really* want as an outcome and the steps are clear. If they have a profound insight or breakthrough, once it is articulated, you want to immediately explore if they are ready to commit to actions based on this new awareness (fig. 9).

When an insight is articulated that relates to achieving the desired outcome, coaching should test if it is time to put the bookend in place. Don't linger. Hesitation and excuses can leak into the process. Turn the insight into a commitment to action by asking a series of questions:

1. What will you do now?
2. By when?
3. What could get in the way of your commitment (which may lead to Plan B or a more realistic plan)?
4. What other support or resources will help?
5. How do you feel about your insights and plans?

When clients share their plans, they feel more obliged to follow through. Commitments become promises. Clients are more

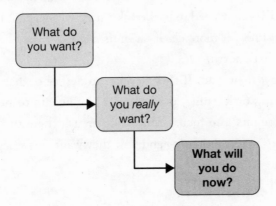

Figure 9. The other bookend: turn insights into commitments.

likely to hold themselves accountable to their words. They are impelled by courage when doubts creep in.

Clients may say they need more time to think about what they now know. Accept they need some time to process their new awareness and ask them what thinking about their revelation looks like. When and where will they take the time to contemplate what they discovered? Ask clients to name at least one next step to ensure they move forward toward their desired outcome.

Clients may tell you they know what to do without planning. Once clients see themselves or the situation differently, they feel they have the answers they need. The new meaning has formed. They feel their next step is obvious. Remember that knowing and doing are not the same. Ask them to say what they are going to do so you both have the same expectation about what happens next. If they don't articulate their intentions, they may still feel tentative after the coaching session ends.[1]

Giving a voice to the insight may feel to you like the right time to move into wrapping up the conversation, but your clients may not be ready. As you move into exploring what to do with the insight, they may need to backtrack a little to sharpen the edges. You will know if more clarification is needed if they hesitate to define what's next.

Follow their lead. If they hesitate to describe what they are now seeing or learning, use reflective statements to help bring their thoughts into focus. You may even ask them to share the new story that is unfolding and how they want this story to end.

END ON A HIGH NOTE

Before the session ends, ask clients to summarize their coaching journey from the start of the session to this moment. Let them describe their experience. If you think they missed an important shift, offer what you recall to acknowledge what else they accomplished. Remind clients of the work they did so they recognize their contribution instead of giving you, the coach, the credit for their growth.

Then, no matter what has occurred during the session, complete the session on the highest note possible, from recognizing they took time out of their busy day for coaching to applauding the courageous steps they took to achieve a breakthrough. If sessions go well, clients will praise you. Don't take the bait. Remind them what *they* did to move forward.

If this is an ongoing relationship, recognize the milestones clients have reached over time. Appreciate them for sticking with the coaching even when they are busy.

As a part of creating closure, choose one or more ways to acknowledge your clients' behaviors and progress at significant moments within and at the end of a session:

1. Describe a moment they were willing to be open or vulnerable that led to a significant shift in the coaching.
2. Recognize their growth since previous sessions.
3. Recall moments when they were willing to be vulnerable that helped them remove a barrier to success.
4. Notice milestones reached and commitments accomplished.

Humans repeat and build on specific behaviors that are positively recognized. You aren't just saying nice things. You are reinforcing your clients' commitment to growth by reminding their brains they can succeed. Because the brain wants to protect us from disappointment, embarrassment, and failure, focusing on what is working, even when progress is slow, gives your clients the rationale their brains need to support risk-taking.

Finally, ask the client to agree the session is over. You can ask, "Are we complete?" or "Do you want to set our next session?" or "Is there anything else you need for now?" You don't need to fill in the time if several minutes are still left on the session clock. Let clients decide what to do with the time. They might appreciate ending early, or they might have another issue they want to address.

You both should feel the uplift of energy when the session ends. Even if your clients' commitment was to spend time contemplating their new awareness because it was jarring, send them off by recognizing their willingness to reflect on what they want to change. Remember, the impact of coaching often happens after the session is over. The shift in perception embeds when clients apply what they learned about themselves to their daily lives.

LIFT UP A LOW NOTE

If at the end of a session, clients question the value of the conversation, acknowledge any progress made on defining the desired outcome or blocks to success. Forward movement in difficult situations often takes more than one session. You might ask them to jot down a few thoughts about the coaching session in a few days and email them to you. Since the best coaching often happens between sessions, their shift in thinking can take a few days to become clear. You can use the notes they send you to springboard the conversation in your next coaching session if they agree to maintain this direction.

If clients feel it is better to end the coaching relationship, acknowledge their honesty and honor their request. You might offer other resources that could be more useful for their immediate needs, such as mentoring, a book, a podcast, or a training program. You might even recommend another coach if they would like a different approach. Remember your purpose is to facilitate their growth, not to keep them as a client as long as you can.

If the ending has come after a long time together, be happy for the next chapter they are beginning. Recall the progress they made with you. Then, wish them well on their journey. Parting ways is inevitable. Don't take it as a personal loss. Like parents letting their children grow up and move on, appreciate your clients' desires to choose new ways to grow.

Three Tips for Articulating Insights and Commitments

Reflective inquiry evokes insight. Yet a new awareness must be made tangible for clients to build on it with actions. Then, the coach must ensure clients' commitment to taking the actions they declare they will do. Use the following tips to help ensure clients can clearly articulate what they have learned about their thinking and then declare their commitment to the actions they intend to take:

1. *Epiphanies trigger emotional shifts.* The shift might be slight, such as when your clients' face goes blank. You might ask, "What just happened?" or "What are you seeing now?" The shift might be more discernable, such as an embarrassed laugh or tears. No matter the intensity of the shift, don't sympathize or try to diminish your clients' reaction. Use silence to allow them to fully experience the moment. When they indicate a readiness to move on, share the shift in emotions you noticed. Follow up by asking, "What does this mean to you?" or "What are you seeing that prompted the shift?" They might need to talk through what they are coming to understand. Give them all the space they need to grasp what has emerged.

2. *Invite clients to choose the direction of the coaching after an important revelation.* Their insight could indicate a new outcome to achieve in the coaching. After an important revelation, invite

clients to choose the direction of the coaching. Are they ready to look at what actions to take now, or do they want to redefine what they want to achieve? If they say they are clear on the actions they want to take, ask how their actions will help them achieve the outcome they agreed to. If they say they want to resolve something else based on what they now understand, ask if they would like to restate what they want to achieve by the end of the session. Let clients choose which path to take.

3. *Turn their intention to change into a commitment to action.* When clients share their plans to act with completion dates, they are more likely to hold themselves accountable to their words. They may say they know what to do, but knowing and doing are not the same. Wrapping up the session with a commitment to do at least one thing, even if it's taking time to reflect on the session, strengthens their conviction to act when doubts or busyness creep in.

PART III

THE THREE MENTAL HABITS

Mastery is the deepening of presence,
not the perfection of skills.

—MARCIA REYNOLDS

WHEN I TEACH leaders how to use a coaching approach to their conversations, I often hear the complaint "I'm asking more questions. No matter what I do, they don't open up to me."

My answer is always, "How are you listening?"

Knowing what to say in a coaching conversation is not enough. Developing coaching skills will help you engage clients to sort out their thoughts and think more clearly for themselves. Going deeper—uncovering what clients really want and what is stopping them from achieving their desires—requires that clients feel safe with you.

Leadership expert Doug Silsbee said, "In fact, our ability to facilitate lasting, sustainable development in others absolutely rests on the presence that we offer to the relationship."[1] In his book *Presence-Based Coaching*, Silsbee defined the power of the relational field. The energy between two people is often referred to as the *atmosphere* or *vibrations* felt. This energy can now be measured.[2]

> The energy you create with your emotions has substance. The relational field is palpable and powerful.

Our nervous system acts as a radio receiver. We pick up the emotional waves of the person we are with. Carl Jung said, "The meeting of two personalities is like the contact of two chemical substances."[3] Something happens in the space between brains when people interact. We either connect or disconnect according to how we feel in each other's presence. We open up or shut down.

This emotional contagion is not equally weighted. The emotions of the socially dominant person in a conversation carry more impact.[4] The coach, unless intimidated by the status of the client, is the socially dominant person in a coaching conversation. Even if you are adept at hiding your emotions, clients will be affected by what you are feeling.

> Because coaching can trigger clients to feel uncertain, vulnerable, and off-balance, you must consciously set and maintain your emotional tone to sustain their sense of safety no matter what emotions they experience.

Your emotions and your regard for your clients will impact their willingness and courage to learn. Clients need to feel psychologically safe with you.

PSYCHOLOGICAL SAFETY

Our brains are attuned to threats. We *sense* danger energetically. The coach's responsibility is to create the conditions for clients to feel safe enough to say what is on their minds. Employee engagement expert William Kahn described psychological safety as "being able to show and employ one's self without fear of negative consequences of self-image, status or career."[5] Coaches are responsible for creating a *safety bubble* where clients feel comfortable being themselves.[6]

> Trust and psychological safety are not the same.

Clients may trust what you say. They may trust you will keep the conversation confidential. They trust you but might not feel safe to fully express themselves to you. They might wonder, "Will

I be ridiculed or made to feel wrong when I share my thoughts?" or "Will I be laughed at if I reveal my fears and yearnings?" The answer to these questions is *no* when clients feel you care, you accept their experience and perspective as valid for them, and you believe they are smart and resourceful enough to find a way forward. Your good intentions are lost if you feel fear, impatience, or judgment.

> Your emotions and positive regard have more impact on how safe clients feel than the words you choose.

In recent years, researchers have been measuring the value of therapeutic presence where therapy patients, including those who have experienced significant trauma, feel safe enough to fully participate in a difficult conversation. *Presence* is described as a neurophysiological state of trust and safety in both client and therapist. The need to protect and defend oneself is regulated down, creating optimal conditions for growth and change.[7]

When practicing therapeutic presence, you don't need to monitor your posture, nonverbal expressions, and voice. Instead, you open your mind, heart, and gut—the three major organs that make up the nervous system—with curiosity, care, and courage. The emotions you feel have more power to establish safety than the placement of your arms. Additionally, the time you spend thinking about opening your arms, positioning your legs, sitting back, looking concerned, or giving eye contact is time you are in your head and not present to the person you are with.

If you open the centers of your nervous system with curiosity, care, and courage and remind yourself of your belief in the other person's potential, it's likely your nonverbal behavior will reflect your sincere interest and acceptance whether you cross your arms or not. You need to manage your inner space to ensure the space around you is engaging and comfortable.

The following chapters will help you implement the three mental habits that provide the psychological safety needed to effectively implement the five practices laid out in part II. To coach with mastery, you need to do the following:

1. Align your brain.
2. Receive (don't just listen).
3. Catch and release judgment.

A story arc is a continuing story line in a book, movie, or television show that is threaded through and unfolds in all chapters and episodes. The ARC of coaching—employing your mental habits—is threaded through all sessions. Practice these three mental habits to masterfully apply your coaching skills.

CHAPTER 8

ALIGN YOUR BRAIN

Attention consists of suspending our thought,
leaving it detached, empty, and ready to be penetrated . . .
waiting, not seeking anything, but ready to receive.

—SIMONE WEIL

A COMMONLY HELD belief is that practice makes perfect and achieving ten thousand hours of practice will grant you mastery. Many studies dispute this.[1] Practice makes any performance, including coaching, easier and more effective, but being fully present while coaching is the critical factor to enter the zone of mastery.

To be fully present requires you develop the habit of being physically and mentally aware in the moment to only what is happening in the coaching interaction. Nothing outside the interaction exists. Thoughts may float through your brain, but they don't stay. We call this *coaching presence.*

The practice of coaching presence has been compared to practicing mindfulness, where you are aware of what is going on inside and outside your mind and body. Developing mindfulness will help you notice when thoughts and sensations in your body occur and then allow them to pass through. When you use mindfulness in coaching, you notice your thoughts and reactions, breathe, and come back to being present to the person you are with. You choose to be curious instead of knowing what the person needs, patient instead of being eager to find solutions, and courageously quiet instead of leaping to help.

Coaching presence has two benefits. First, you are able to receive what clients express in words and expressions. Second, your open presence creates the psychological safety needed to have an honest, exploratory conversation.

The following three steps will help you align your brain:

1. Choose how you want to feel
2. Recall your intention of partnership
3. Believe in your client's potential

Establishing your presence by aligning your brain before you engage in a coaching conversation is important. Your presence creates a safe and open atmosphere even more than your words. Then you must maintain your alignment, readjusting your brain when necessary during your conversation. When you get distracted by your own thoughts, quickly shift back to being present.

CHOOSE HOW YOU WANT TO FEEL

Because your emotions have more impact than your words, you must consciously choose how you want to feel before you meet with your client. You don't just think about how you want to feel; you deliberately shift your physical state by breathing in the emotions you want to feel. Flood your body with emotions by choice.

In 1998, I was asked to create a program for professionals to find their zone of excellence based on studying what top athletes do to perform well under pressure. I reviewed research in sports psychology and interviewed top athletes in six sports on how to master the art of being present. I found the best competitors do not think about anything, not even winning, when they perform *in the zone*. Thinking of winning causes their brains to entertain the possibility of losing. Instead, the champions cleared their minds, allowing their bodies to freely move as they enjoyed doing what they most loved.[2]

This mental state is called *flow* and is characterized by complete absorption in what one is doing, losing a sense of time and space, where nothing else matters. Mihaly Csikszentmihalyi, the psychologist who named the concept of flow, defined the experience as an optimal state of consciousness where we perform at our best while enjoying the moment. Csikszentmihalyi said that in this state, we know what is going on but "react to it in a reflexive, instinctive way. . . . We can deliberately weigh what the senses tell us and respond accordingly."[3] Thinking isn't necessary.

Csikszentmihalyi's work led to countless studies and writings about mindfulness and the impact of emotions on our results. In most of this work, emotions were the result of entering flow. Other researchers have since suggested that recalling emotions, such as compassion or peacefulness, can help us enter the flow state. Based on studies of emotional intelligence, we now know many emotions can trigger the biochemical changes that produce a sense of flow. Some of these emotions are happiness, contentment, love, gratitude, appreciation, and curiosity.

When I asked the athletes how they felt when in flow, they said they felt peaceful and confident. Some said they felt gratitude. They hadn't thought about it, but yes, they felt their emotions were significant in keeping them in a state of flow. If they fell into fear, they fell out of flow.

To get into the flow of coaching, you don't just clear your mind; you choose one or two emotions you want to feel throughout the conversation. You might choose to be curious and caring, calm and courageous, or grateful and optimistic. You choose what emotions will help you stay present. Your choices could change when you consider the needs of each client. At the end of this chapter you will find a four-step Presencing Routine to infuse these emotions into your body.[4]

Being present while coaching builds rapport. Not only do you hear more words and notice even small emotional shifts, but your clients feel safer with you. The energy from your emotions adds a positive dynamic to your conversations.

The art of being present while practicing your skills takes patience. You are overcoming a lifetime of distracting mental habits. As your presence matures, so will your contentment when working with clients.

RECALL YOUR INTENTION OF PARTNERSHIP

Clients must sense that your intention is to partner with them to discover the best way forward throughout the conversation. As soon as you shift your intention to wanting them to go in a particular direction you think is best for them, their safety is impaired, if not lost. If they don't actively resist your coaching, their brain activity decreases.

You must let their thoughts have a life of their own. You may sense their blocks before they do and hope they decide on specific actions and outcomes, but you never lose sight that the journey is theirs to take. You are their thinking partner. They choose the direction, clarify the options, and make the decisions.

> The moment clients feel you are leading them to a specific conclusion, they will resist you, passively comply, or mentally check out.

Clients must know you are coaching to help them work through their dilemmas, not to persuade them to do what is right. They must know you trust their intelligence and serve their higher good, not your own. This intention helps them feel safe, even when they feel vulnerable.

To maintain your intention of partnership, choose to feel open and curious to what will unfold. You are listening for thinking patterns to examine together, not answers that match your beliefs. You are curious about their assumptions, not judging whether they are right or wrong. As they search for evidence to support their beliefs, you may notice contradictions in their reasoning. With reflective statements, questions, and moments of silence, trust they will adequately question their own thinking. They will trust you in return.

Remember, your intention isn't to get somewhere, fix their problem, or make them into someone else. You are their thinking partner. Your purpose is to broaden their perspective to find the answers they probably knew all along.

BELIEVE IN YOUR CLIENT'S POTENTIAL

Humanistic psychologist Abraham Maslow said feeling cared about, accepted, and respected is necessary before we can realize our full potential of consciousness and creativity. We long to be heard, be understood, and feel significant. We must be seen by others before we can know ourselves.

These days, with our eyes glued to phones and computers, we don't see each other. We barely know each other much less accept each other for the unique, amazing beings we are. Our habits squeeze out time for establishing real connections. We have little tolerance for conversations that go beneath the surface.

We all seek the safety to be who we are in the company of others. This safety is lost when you jump to fix problems, assuage emotions, or try to persuade clients to feel empowered. These actions reflect your belief they are inadequate. If their brains detect even a likelihood that the conversation will feel patronizing or contrived, they become defensive or mentally retreat. Connection is lost.

> When you lose your belief in your clients' ability to discover their own way forward, they are no longer a fully respected partner in the conversation.

Not believing in people's potential to solve their own problems creates what journalist Johann Hari calls *parodies of connection* where the humanity in people is invisible when we interact.[5] In coaching, the power dynamics shift away from partnering. Clients leave conversations feeling betrayed or frustrated. This makes future attempts at connecting even harder. You both lose when you give in to your urge to fix your clients' problems.

People must feel valued to fully engage and be open to growing. The sense of significance we feel when we know others value who we are and what we do fuels our motivation when facing difficult dilemmas. Therefore, your belief in your clients' potential, that they are creative, resourceful, and whole, is critical to the outcome.

> You don't empower people by giving them tasks and homework. Personal power comes from within, when people feel seen, cared about, and respected.

Practice seeing potential in all people you interact with. The next people you meet, look them in the eye. No matter if you agree with what they are saying, honor the human in front of you, knowing they are doing their best to survive and succeed with what they know. Hopefully, you can help them realize what else they can know.

KEY POINTS TO REMEMBER

The following list highlights the key points to remember about aligning your brain to create the energetic bond needed to successfully coach the person, not the problem:

- Presence gives you the awareness of what is occurring in yourself, in the person you are with, and in the space between you.
- You need to take three steps to groom your brain before a coaching conversation to establish a sense of psychological safety: (1) choose how you want to feel, (2) recall your intention of partnership, and (3) believe in the client's potential.
- The emotions you choose to feel before and during the coaching conversation have more impact on the outcome than your words.
- If you are truly there to help clients think, you must let their thoughts have a mind of their own. Remain open and curious to what unfolds.
- Coaching conversations require you feel respect for the human in front of you to inspire their willingness to learn

and grow. See them, value their existence, and believe in their potential.

Practice aligning your brain regularly until this mental state feels natural. Align your brain before you start your day, when you prepare for any conversation, before you sit down to answer emails, and as you prepare for having a good night's sleep. You can then control your mind when your emotions are triggered.

Creating the Habit of Aligning Your Brain: Presencing Routine

Use this four-step Presencing Routine to align your brain before a coaching conversation and anytime you are distracted by your thoughts and emotions.

The four steps consist of the following:

1. Relax your body.
2. Detach from the thoughts in your head.
3. Center your awareness.
4. Focus on the emotion you want to feel.

Step 1. Relax Your Body

You must release the tension in your body before you can clear your mind and shift your emotions.

Stress from daily functions shows up in your body. Your muscles tighten, your breathing stops or slows down, your jaw clenches, your stomach churns, and your shoulders move toward your ears.

Telling yourself to calm down helps only for a few seconds. You must actively shift your biological state before you can control what is going on in your brain.

First, focus on your breath. When stressed, you stop or shorten your breathing. The quickest way to relieve stress is to exhale and then let your breathing return to a normal, easy rhythm.

Next, release any tension you are holding in your neck, back, arms, and legs. If you know where you tend to hold tension, go there. Breathe in and relax those spots. If you aren't sure where to focus, do a quick body scan, releasing tension in each part of your body. Start with your forehead and jaw; then move to your shoulders, chest, stomach, arms, and legs. Breathe and release your tension at various times throughout the day. You will have more energy when you need it.

To sustain relaxation, regularly engage in activities that release tension. Try meditation, yoga, or other calming practices. Participate in fun team sports. Do exercises you enjoy. Go dancing. Seek an activity that evokes pleasure and gratitude, such as walking in the park or hiking in the desert, playing with your children or pets, or making time in your schedule for your favorite hobby.

My favorite form of a quick tension reliever is looking at my "favorite pictures" album on my cell phone. The joy and gratitude I feel instantly spreads a sense of well-being throughout my body.

You can also deliberately slow down your life. Eat more slowly, drive more leisurely, and walk at a gentler pace. To consistently clear your mind, lighten up your body.

Step 2. Detach from the Thoughts in Your Head

After you relax your body, free up your mind by detaching from the chatter in your brain. Clean out the clutter—your worries about your impact as a coach, fears around the ongoing relationship, and troubles outside of coaching. You can enter the flow state of coaching only with a clear mind.

You can see this phenomenon at work when you do something just for the fun of it. When you have nothing to lose, you're likely to do your best. You deliver a top-notch speech, dance with abandon, or write an inspiring piece.

Start your practice of detaching by stopping your thoughts for one minute while observing the world around you. If your mind drifts or you start judging, analyzing, or evaluating, let your thoughts float away. Return to noticing the details of the world around you for sixty seconds.

Tomorrow, increase your practice to two minutes. Each day see how much longer you can go before your brain fills up with thoughts.

Step 3. Center Your Awareness

Many Eastern philosophies teach that the true center of the mind lies in the center of the body. To get there, you move your awareness out of your head and down into your core—an act known as *centering*.

Athletes, performers, and martial artists are taught to move their awareness to their diaphragm or a spot just below the navel. Some people find their center by noticing the bottom of their breath when filling their belly with air. I teach my students to recall a moment in their life when they stood or spoke up despite their fears and then notice the strength emanating from the center of their bodies. Feeling courageous—having guts—opens the center of your body.

Once a day, take a few moments to close your eyes, breathe deeply, and notice the center of your body. Keep your awareness there for as long as you can.

When you are comfortable keeping your awareness out of your head and at your center, add a variety of activities to your practice. Play sports, read, listen to music, or hike while focusing your awareness on the center of your body. From this new perspective, you'll begin to see and hear more details. You will move with both strength and calmness.

Then you can take centering into your social interactions. Just the act of speaking and listening from your center builds rapport with others. They feel safer with you. They will hear what you say more clearly.

Whenever you are having difficulty staying present, place one hand lightly on your belly and tap your fingers. This brings your attention out of your head and into your body. Remind yourself to breathe.

As with all new habits, centering requires daily practice. Give yourself time to master it. Start your practice in nonthreatening situations. Stay consistent with daily practice so centering becomes a habit instead of a technique.

Step 4. Focus on the Emotion You Want to Feel

After relaxing, detaching, and centering, choose one or two emotions you want to feel while coaching. Consider how you want your clients to feel at the end of your interaction. Do you want them to feel hopeful, encouraged, curious, or proud? You might choose to feel the way you want your clients to feel while coaching.

Before I coach, I breathe in the feelings "curious and care." I have these words on a piece of paper within my range of vision. If I get flustered or feel the urge to advise, I glance at my paper. I breathe in and feel curious and care for my client. The right words always show up.

CHAPTER 9

RECEIVE (DON'T JUST LISTEN)

*Real listening is a willingness to let
the other person change you.*

—ALAN ALDA

I FIRST HEARD the word *receive* used as a form of listening when I watched Julian Treasure's viral TED Talk, "5 Ways to Listen Better."[1] His formula for listening is RASA, which stands for receive, appreciate, summarize, and ask. When I deliver one- or two-day Courageous Coaching workshops for leaders, I teach them this formula as a way to use a coaching approach in their leadership conversations. They do exercises to experience what fully receiving and appreciating the talker's perspective feels like. Most admit they struggled with not jumping in to give advice, but the concept of receiving without judgment and appreciating the person's experience helped the leaders stay present. Then, adding in the requirement to summarize and ask only clarifying questions forces them to focus their attention on the person they are listening to.

> Receiving the person fully, not just listening to them, is critical for using reflective inquiry to coach the person, not the problem.

The act of receiving means you take in what clients offer you. You hear their words, notice their shifts in expression and posture, catch the subtle shifts in emotion, and sense when there is something they haven't said. When you accept and honor people for who they are and what they are experiencing, they are more likely to open up and explore with you.

LISTENING TO

In your daily interactions, the intention behind listening is usually to gain information that will fulfill your needs. You keep your distance from the other person by staying in your head, even when you say your intention is to collaborate. The person feels little connection with you when you part.

You *listen to* people for these purposes:

1. *To collect data.* You listen to know what to say or do next. Outside of coaching, you listen to formulate your argument, to compare your perspective to others', or to refine your own point of view if you feel you are missing something. When coaching, you listen until you feel you have enough information to jump in and explore options.

2. *To give an answer or solve a problem.* You listen to know what advice to give once others fully share their story.

3. *To obey protocol.* You listen because it is the right thing to do, generally for the minimal amount of time you think it takes for people to think you care. You listen because you should, not because you want to.

Cognitive Awareness

Listening to people requires you to use cognitive awareness. You seek to understand what people are saying, interpreting what you hear.

You might notice emotional shifts in their expression, but your tendency will be to analyze their reactions, even though it is hard to accurately decipher facial expressions.[2] Far more is going on in any interaction than what people are saying and perceptibly expressing.

Using only cognitive awareness focuses on collecting data to understand clients' story from their point of view. Cognitive listening often leads to diagnosing problems to find solutions. The coaching skims the surface in search of options and consequences.

RECEIVING

When you choose to be present and connect with someone, you listen beyond your analytical brain. You open your nervous system to receive with your heart and gut as well as with your open mind. The person feels heard, valued, and possibly transformed as a result.[3]

Receiving requires you to suspend analysis. You take in and accept people's words, expressions, and emotions as elements of their experience. You acknowledge the story they offer as valid from their current point of view. You don't insert your opinions or judgments.

You *receive* what people offer for these purposes:

1. *To connect with the other people.* You listen to establish a connection. You stay present throughout the conversation, receiving more than their words and nonverbal gestures. You resist the urge to know what is coming next. Your clients appreciate your ease with not knowing.

2. *To let people know you value them.* You listen so clients feel heard, understood, and valued. Also, you expand your capacity for empathy when you value what people tell you, even when your perspective differs from theirs.

3. *To strengthen your relationship.* You listen for the purpose of being with others. We often enjoy friends this way. Can you listen to clients as if they were dear friends?

4. *To explore, learn, and grow together.* You listen with curiosity to learn from the amazing human in front of you. You enjoy when the conversation takes you somewhere new and unexpected. Connecting with others this way is the same connection you sense when you view an awesome sunset, gaze across a beautiful canyon, or watch a shooting star fall and disappear into the black of night.[4] Letting go of what you know lets you observe the magic of coaching even while you are coaching.

Receiving is an active, not passive, act. To fully receive, you need to be aware of your sensory reactions as well as your mental activity. With sensory awareness, you can receive and discern what is going on with others beyond the words they speak.

Sensory Awareness

Sensory awareness includes an inward awareness of your reactions in a conversation. Your reactions might be in response to what clients tell you. You also might be reacting to what you energetically receive from them.

You can sense people's desires, disappointments, needs, frustrations, hopes, and doubts when they can't or have trouble articulating these experiences themselves. This requires you to access all three processing centers of the nervous system—your brain, heart, and gut. A visualization on how to open all three of these processing centers is presented in the exercise at the end of this chapter.

Being sensitive doesn't mean being wishy-washy. It means you are aware of what is going on around you on a sensory level. You can sense when people are conflicted, distressed, or stimulated. Most people claim their pets have this uncanny ability to sense their emotional needs. Humans can receive these emotional vibrations as well. We just don't pay attention to them.

You were likely taught to ignore your sensory awareness as a part of your conditioning as a child. Were you ever told, "You shouldn't take things so personally" or "You should toughen up"? This led you to rely on your cognitive brain for listening and interpreting meaning.

When you don't allow people to get under your skin, you aren't experiencing them fully. You are disconnected internally and externally. You put up a wall between yourself and the people you are with.

I'm often asked if venturing into the land of emotions is risky, especially at work. I hear, "I can't allow people's emotions to sway me." The business world is full of aphorisms that declare, "Only the tough survive."

> When you allow yourself to be sensitive—to experience others enough to sense what they are feeling—your reflective statements have more impact.

You can gain some understanding of what clients are experiencing by noticing their body language and voice, but you gain a deeper awareness when you pick up the emotional energy vibrating between you.[5] You might feel this energy in your heart or gut. You grasp when clients want you to back off and give them space, quietly standing by. You know when they are impatient to move on or if they want to spend more time on a topic. You can tell when they just want to be heard or if they want to be acknowledged for doing the best they can with what they have right now.

You might feel their stress, anxiety, and anger in your body. If you let these emotions sit in your body, you won't be able to effectively coach. Empathy is where you receive what another is feeling using sensory awareness, but when coaching, you need to let these sensations pass through you. As described in chapter 4, you can then experience *nonreactive empathy*. You share what you saw, heard, and felt with your clients. If you felt their emotion, you relax your body and let the emotion subside as you return to being fully present with them.

> Receive and then offer your clients what you see, hear, and feel to help them better understand the experience. Release their emotions so you can hold a safe space for them to process your offering.

Practice aligning your brain to stay present with curiosity, care, and the belief in clients' potential. Receive what they offer without analysis or judgment. Share what you receive. Release the emotions you sensed they felt. Your presence encourages connection, safety, and the openness to discover a new way forward together.

Five Steps for Building Sensory Awareness in Conversation

Practice these steps for keeping your brain clear while coaching. You will be able to clearly receive your clients' words and expressions and offer them back for their consideration:

1. *Be quiet, inside and out.* When you quiet your thinking and chattering brain, you clear your sensory channels.

2. *Let go of knowing.* Instead of thinking you know how your clients will react, try believing anything can happen. You might be surprised. Unfortunately, the better you know someone, the more likely you will quit being curious. Can you release knowing what people will say when you ask them a question?

3. *Release the need to be right.* Be curious and ask questions to understand your clients' perspective. After you share what you receive, accept their response. If they disagree, go with their interpretation. They may need time and space to think about what they feel.

4. *Listen with your heart and gut as well as your head.* Before your conversation, open your heart with feelings of compassion or gratitude. Then, open your gut by feeling your courage. Use the visualization on the next page to help you develop this habit.

5. *Test your instinct.* When you feel a sensation in your heart or gut, share what you think your clients might be feeling, such as anger, frustration, sadness, or yearning. Accept their response whether they agree with you or not. If you are wrong, your guess could help them name the emotions they are feeling.

A. H. Almaas said, "Therefore, the more accustomed we are to the inner stillness and peacefulness, the more perceptive we become on the subtle dimensions. This can take our inquiry to deeper levels, to a newer kind of knowledge, to a different kind of experience."[6]

Creating the Habit of Receiving: Full-Body Presence

The following visualization exercise will help you open your head, heart, and gut before your next conversation. Pause between the steps.

1. Sit in a chair and become a witness to your body. Soften your gaze and shift it downward. Notice how your body feels. Shift your position to feel comfortable while sitting upright.

2. Feel where your body is making contact with the chair. Feel where you have placed your feet.

3. Notice your emotional state. Do you feel sad? Calm? Tired? Impatient? Whatever you feel, see if you can relax and release it so you become open to the process you are about to step into.

4. Focus on your breathing. Feel your body respond as your breath moves in and out. Feel the temperature of the air as you inhale it into your body. Let your body relax as the air flows out. If you notice specific spots of tension relating to your emotions, breathe into these spots. As you breathe out, let the tension flow out of your body.

5. Bring your awareness into your brain. Picture an elevator sitting in the center of your mind. The door is open. Allow your thoughts, judgments, and opinions to float into the empty elevator. When they are safely inside, see the door close, leaving your mind free of thoughts. Say the word "curious" to yourself. Breathe in and feel how curiosity opens your mind.

6. Return to the elevator in your mind. The door is still closed. Watch the elevator float slowly down your body, through your neck, and into your chest, and see it settle in the spot next to your heart. Recall someone or a pet you deeply care about. Or maybe you see a scene that opens your heart. As the elevator door opens,

see the person, pet, or place that fills you with gratitude, happiness, or love. Take a deep breath in, and say the word you feel, such as "love," "happy," or "grateful." Feel your heart expand.

7. Return to the elevator next to your heart. Say goodbye to the person, pet, or place as the door closes. See the elevator float slowly down your body, down your center, and come to rest at the spot just below your navel. A warm glow is coming from the elevator door. When the door opens, there is nothing inside but the warm glow. Feel the warmth of this glow. Recall a time you felt gutsy and determined—a time you spoke up or did something despite your fear. Remember how you felt as you took action or spoke your mind. As you inhale, say the word "courage" to yourself. Let the word settle into the center of your body before you exhale. Keep breathing with your mind on your center, your point of strength.

8. Now, open your eyes. Take your open head, heart, and gut with you as you coach or engage in any conversation.

After your next coaching session, consider if you had a difficult time accessing one part of the nervous system. I've heard, "I can do the gut, but listening to my heart feels awkward" and "I am always listening with my heart. Sharing what I sense from my gut feels scary." People who tend to be helpers listen more easily from their heart than their gut. Risk-takers who move quickly on instinct find it easier to listen from their gut than their heart. In your daily interactions, practice receiving from your most vulnerable place to balance the three large organs of your nervous system. This practice will help you open and align your entire nervous system when coaching.

CHAPTER 10

CATCH AND RELEASE JUDGMENT

*Coaching gives people a safe space to be themselves,
with all their emotions and moods.*

—MARCIA REYNOLDS

I WAS COACHING a man in China in front of a big audience. He wanted to explore if he should be a coach when he retired. I asked him what he loved about his job being the director of human resources for his company. He told me he loved developing people. He loved seeing the light in their eyes when they realized they could be so much more than they imagined. Most of all, he was proud he could instill the principles of Communism in them. I felt my entire body shudder. Not only did his political values conflict with mine, but the word *Communism* dredged up horror stories of nuclear attacks emblazoned in my brain as a child. But it wasn't my place to judge or change him. I noticed my reaction, breathed out, and returned to being fully present with this wonderful man who loved seeing the light of possibility shine in people's eyes.

The most common lie accomplished coaches tell themselves is "I am not judgmental." We like to think we are inclusive and non-reactive. Although we may be able to notice when we get caught up in our thoughts and emotions and shift back to being present, we can't help being biased and judgmental. One of the most detrimental yet overlooked emotions we experience is judgment.

Like fear and anger, judgment is an emotional reaction that taints our thoughts. When we hear words and see actions, our brains scan for threats, and then we react. Judgment is a reaction that occurs when the brain determines that what was said or done conflicts with our frames—who we think we are (identity) and how the world should work (reality). No matter how present we think we are being, our brains are still at work discerning contradictions to what we think is right, wrong, good, and bad. This makes us all judgmental by nature.

Our brains operate with a negativity bias that causes us to register even innocent expressions as negative more readily than neutral or positive.[1] We compare our beliefs against what we think other people believe and then exaggerate the variances out of self-protection. The words we then speak, including the questions we ask, are slanted by our negative interpretations.

> What you believe is important, what you value as right, and how you believe others should act lead to judgment.

Without consciousness, your gestures or words might indicate dissatisfaction. Vincent Van Gogh wrote, "Let's not forget that small emotions are the great captains of our lives, and that these we obey without knowing it." You might lift one eyebrow, scratch your scalp, or replay what clients said but end the sentence with an upward inflection so it sounds like a question instead of a statement. The intention of your follow-up question is to edit their words. Left unchecked, even slight judgmental reactions affect the power dynamic of the relationship, impairing the trust and safety vital to effectively coach the person in front of you. When your judgment seeps through, partnership is lost.

> To release judgment, you must accept that you are judgmental.

Mastery in coaching requires that you accept you are a judgy, biased person. To judge is human. You must recognize and release your judgmental reactions before they sabotage your coaching.

Some of your judgments are easy to catch. Others are unconscious, meaning you aren't aware you reacted negatively to what you heard. These judgments are often referred to as unconscious biases.[2] You frequently judge social behavior, such as how people walk down aisles, what pets they choose, how they dress, and how they talk. You might not notice when you offend people, interrupt, or ignore them, even though you hate when people do this to you. You tell people you didn't intend to offend them, but your intention doesn't matter. They feel slighted anyway.

Unconscious biases are also called *blind spots*. If you would like to have more peace in your life and improve the quality of your relationships, including those with strangers standing in line with you, practice noticing your emotion of judgment to bring some of your unconscious biases to light.

Because unconscious biases are difficult to uncover, allowing someone else to help reveal them to you is helpful. You might have a friend you trust who can point out when one of your biases appears. I have a friend who lets me know when I make snarky remarks. As much as I don't like my judgments pointed out, I am grateful for the awareness. You can also hire a coach to unearth what you blindly defend.

BEYOND FACE VALUE

The most common judgmental reactions happen in response to your clients' emotional reactions. Even a small show of displeasure with their emotional state will affect the progress of the session. Without exploring their reaction, you can easily misjudge the meaning. The practice of catching and releasing your judgment about their emotions will help both you and your clients come to understand the significance of their expressions.

Reactions that are commonly misunderstood include the following:

1. *Nervous laughter.* Laughter is often seen as making light of a situation, yet some people laugh when they feel embarrassed or self-conscious. Yale psychologist Oriana Aragon says nervous laughter is a form of emotional balancing, like when we cry when we are happy.[3] Instead of asking clients what they think is funny or assuming they are ready to move on, ask what their laughter means for them in this moment. You can say something like, "You're laughing. What just came up for you?"

2. *Change in eye contact.* Looking away or holding a steely gaze doesn't mean clients are resisting you. You may have touched on a truth that hasn't been spoken. With acceptance and curiosity, ask clients if they are willing to share their thoughts.

3. *Easy, quick agreement.* You make a reflection and your client quickly replies, "You're right" or "I see what you mean." Be careful not to judge the response as definitive. Like nervous laughter, clients might be trying to escape an uncomfortable truth. Ask them what they think is right or what they now understand.

4. *Tears.* Crying doesn't always mean someone feels hurt or sad. Tears could be a physiological result of stress or a buildup of disappointments. Allow clients to take a moment when tears come to their eyes. Calmly wait for them to signal they are ready to move on. Generally, if you calmly sit in silence, they will let you know when they're ready to talk. If the crying is uncontrollable, offer to reschedule the session but only as a last resort. It is always better to give clients a moment to regain control than to make them feel weak for crying. Once their emotions even out, you might ask if they are comfortable talking about what triggered their tears.

5. *Defensiveness.* Defensiveness is a natural reaction to information clients didn't want to hear. People don't like to feel they did something wrong. They might reflexively defend themselves, get angry, or shut down. Ask what is difficult for them to hear or accept. If there is no risk of physical harm, let them vent to release the steam. Stay compassionately curious. Defensiveness usually subsides if you don't fuel the fire.

6. *Hesitation.* Hesitation is often interpreted as a lack of commitment by clients. It could also be a result of fear of taking a risk, concern over how other people will judge them when they change, or the effect a change might have on their own identity ("Who will I be if I do this?").[4] Reflect the hesitation you notice and ask what is holding them back. They might reveal something that alters the course of the coaching.

RELEASING YOUR "I" FROM YOUR CONVERSATIONS

To be a nonreactive thinking partner, strive to remove *I* from your conversation. If you fully immerse yourself in the conversation and resist the need to tell your opinion or story, you can maintain a strong connection with your client.

Releasing your *I* is difficult because it is a part of the perspective that helps you navigate life, but if you allow your opinions and judgment to fade into the background, you can experience the flow state of coaching. You will still experience emotional reactions. You just won't get caught up in the web of opinions and judgments your *I* wants to interject.

Try walking around for twenty minutes noticing your world without your *I* getting in the way. See if you can notice things, situations, and people as if you had never seen them before. What nuances do you notice? What observations trigger your curiosity? What details open your heart? We miss so much when our *I* leads us through life.

Even with practice, you will probably vacillate between thinking from your *I* state and releasing it as you develop presence and awareness. Releasing your *I* is an aspirational state. The more you coach from this position, the quicker and more profound the results.

WITNESSING YOUR JUDGMENT

Your judgment has many faces. In addition to reacting to clients' emotions or beliefs, you are judging your clients as inadequate when you give them unsolicited advice. When they list multiple concerns, choosing the direction of the conversation for them is a judgment. If you want people to think more broadly for themselves, and you believe they can, you must catch the moments you fall out of being their thinking partner and slip into being the "holder of the truth" where you subtly become the expert wanting to direct the conversation.

The mental habit you want to cultivate is to catch your judgment as an emotional reaction. When you can catch the sensation of judgment as a physiological reaction, you can then breathe out, release the tension, and choose to return to being fully present. My pang of judgment hits my diaphragm at the center spot between my lowest ribs. Sometimes I can feel the tightness rise into my chest and throat, as if trying to escape out my mouth.

I don't always catch my judgment before I speak. My words and reactions are tained by my biases. So I am practicing sensing when opinions seep into my words. Shifting back to partnership when I fall out is better than ignoring what I did. I quickly take back my words by saying, "Sorry, let me rephrase that." Then I attempt to reflect what was said before my interruption. I allow them to correct me if I am wrong. I might then ask if they want to explore how their perspective is affecting their desired outcome, but I'm careful to do this out of curiosity, not the desire to influence.

Judgment is so common, we tend to miss the triggering moments. To help you discern where in your body you feel judgment, follow the steps outlined in the exercise at the end of this chapter. You can also intentionally trigger your judgment to recognize the sensation. Watch or read the news, read Facebook posts, or try to navigate crowded environments to willfully activate your judgment. Then practice releasing the tension to clear your mind.

KEY POINTS TO PRACTICE

Follow these tips to help you develop the mental habit of suspending judgment:

1. *Stop and notice if you are feeling judgment.* Work on discovering how the emotion of judgment shows up in your body so you can catch it before it infects your thoughts.

2. *Don't criticize yourself for judging.* You will have instinctual reactions to people because of their looks, age, political or religious views, sexual preference, disabilities, rude behavior, and criticism of you. Judging is a human reaction. Don't get angry with yourself or lose your confidence. What you courageously choose to do once you notice your judgment is more important than trying to be judgment-free.

3. *Question your assumptions and opinions.* What belief is driving your reactions? Don't rationalize your reaction; just wonder where it came from.

4. *Release your need to be right or have the last word.* Remember, your clients need to feel heard and accepted. Unless their views will impact the outcome they want to create, breathe and release your reaction. If you think what they said will stand in the way of their outcome, ask them to restate what they want to achieve. Then, you can ask if what they shared is in alignment with their outcome or could be a barrier to achieving what they want.

5. *Strive to be more curious about people every day.* Enjoy looking beyond what you think so you can discover something new. Remember, people are acting out of their frames. You don't have to agree with their points of view, but you can openly listen to understand their perspective. You will gain peace of mind and improve your interactions.

We are all big judging machines. And as humans, we can expand our points of view. I wish for a world full of people choosing to see beyond their biases. I hope you wish for that too.

Creating the Habit of Catching and Releasing Your Emotions, Including Judgment: Emotional Recognition

In all situations, not just coaching, the more adept you are at discerning the emotions that are shaping your moods and affecting your thoughts, the greater your ability to shift to feeling something else more conducive to the moment. You can choose what you want to feel instead of reacting in the moment by cultivating the mental habit of emotional recognition.

Putting a name on what you're feeling is often hard because you probably were never trained to do this. Also, you may be experiencing more than one emotion at a time. Not only do emotions overlap and blend, but you can attribute many words to the variations of your reactions, which makes emotional awareness a difficult skill to master. Although the skill is difficult, it is not impossible if you practice these two steps:

1. Stop and notice your emotional state.

2. Name what you are feeling.

The first step to increase your emotional recognition is to stop what you are doing and do a body check. Are you holding tension anywhere? Is your jaw clenched, are your shoulders tight, is your stomach churning, or is your breathing shallow? How are you holding your arms, hands, legs, and feet? Ask yourself what emotions could be causing the tension.

Even if you can't name your sensations, the practice of discerning differences in your physical and mental states is a good start. Most people don't recognize shifts in their emotions throughout the day. They just know they feel tired, frustrated, or content at the end of the day.

If you deliberately stop what you are doing at least three times a day and ask yourself, "What am I feeling?" you can begin to create a habit of emotional recognition. After at least three weeks of this practice, you will more naturally notice shifts in what you feel throughout your day.

As you continue your practice, you will improve your ability to notice your emotional reactions while coaching. Then you can align your brain using the Presencing Routine you learned in chapter 8: relax, detach, center, and focus on feeling curiosity and care to return to being present with your client.

For the next three weeks, set your phone or watch to alarm or vibrate four times throughout the day to check in on how you are feeling. It's important to assess what you are feeling *in the moment* instead of relying on memory. Change the intervals each week so you aren't checking at the same time each day. Track your emotions on paper or digitally so you can check if you notice any patterns to the emotions you feel.

Start with identifying some basic emotions. Determine if you are feeling angry, frustrated, impatient, judgy, irritated, anxious, disgusted, disappointed, sad, surprised, determined, happy, or content. You may be feeling more than one emotion at a time. See if you can identify the physical sensations of your emotions. If you isolate the feeling in your body, you can choose how to act even as you feel. The emotions will then subside, making it easier to shift your emotions by choice.

After a few weeks of stopping your activity and naming your emotions, try to discern variations in your emotions beyond the basics. Use the list in table 1 to help you expand your emotional vocabulary.

Remember, you are seeking to be more aware of all your feelings. They are not right or wrong. Therefore, honesty is important. After at least three weeks of practicing emotional recognition, you should be able to continue without an alarm.

The goal of the practice is to create the mental habit of catching your emotional reactions when they occur. This gives you the opportunity to then choose to feel something else if you want to. Choose to be the master of your mind, not the victim of your reactions.

Table 1. Feelings/Inventory

Related to	Feelings		
Anger	Furious	Outraged	Hateful
	Resentful	Exasperated	Annoyed
	Irritated	Vengeful	Cheated
	Belligerent	Rebellious	Resistant
	Envious	Superior	Defiant
	Disdainful	Repulsed	Appalled
	Offended	Distrustful	Cynical
	Wary	Concerned	Apprehensive
Fear	Nervous	Dreading	Worried
	Afraid	Anxious	Edgy
	Restless	Frightened	Threatened
	Stressed	Overwhelmed	Obsessed
Disheartenment	Confused	Baffled	Lost
	Disoriented	Disconnected	Trapped
	Lonely	Isolated	Sad
	Grieving	Dejected	Gloomy
	Desperate	Depressed	Devastated
	Helpless	Weak	Vulnerable
	Moody	Serious	Somber
	Disappointed	Hurt	Defective
	Shy	Unloved	Abandoned
	Frail	Queasy	Weary
	Tired	Burned out	Apathetic

continued

Table 1. (continued)

Related to	Feelings		
Disheartenment (continued)	Complacent	Bored	Brainless
	Exhausted	Frustrated	Grumpy
	Impatient	Testy	Wound up
Shame	Humiliated	Mortified	Embarrassed
	Ashamed	Uncomfortable	Guilty
	Regretful	Remorseful	Reflective
	Sorrowful	Detached	Aloof
Surprise	Shocked	Startled	Stunned
	Amazed	Astonished	Impressed
Passion	Enthusiastic	Excited	Aroused
	Delirious	Passionate	Crazed
	Euphoric	Thrilled	Competitive
	Willful	Determined	Confident
	Bold	Eager	Optimistic
	Gratified	Proud	Gushy
Happiness	Joyful	Blissful	Amused
	Delighted	Triumphant	Lucky
	Pleased	Silly	Dreamy
	Enchanted	Appreciative	Grateful
	Hopeful	Intrigued	Interested
	Engrossed	Alive	Vivacious
Calm	Contented	Relieved	Peaceful
	Relaxed	Satisfied	Reserved
	Comfortable	Receptive	Forgiving
	Accepting	Loved	Serene
Care	Adoring	Admiring	Reverent
	Loving	Affectionate	Supportive
	Respectful	Friendly	Sympathetic
	Compassionate	Tender	Generous

Other:

(Write in your own)

BEYOND THE CONVERSATION

Coaching as a Lifestyle and a Culture

*Who we are and what we do
are so tightly connected.*

—HERMINIA IBARRA

A YEAR AFTER I started my coach training, I was at lunch with a group of friends I had known for years. During the meal, one of them said, "Marcia, I want you to know how enjoyable you are to be with these days." I sort of smiled and then asked what she meant. "It just feels so much more comfortable talking to you." I tilted my head, prompting her to go on. "Well, like now, you listen more. I don't know, you just seem more interested in us. Don't get me wrong—you're so smart, you always have good advice. And you tell great stories! But something has changed in you. I just wanted to let you know." Everyone at the table agreed. My closest friend sensed my discomfort, lifted her glass to get everyone to toast our friendship, and changed the subject to a new restaurant she found that we should try out next month.

Those words haunted me for days. Was I an awful friend before? I disliked people who jumped in to give me advice before I could finish talking. Had I been the person that most frustrated me?

After days of exhaustive contemplation, I woke up thinking, "Well, they are still my friends. They call me when they have big problems to solve. They miss me when work gets in the way of our being together. So, I forgive myself for being a know-it-all in the past and thank God I found coaching!" That's when I realized my coaching habits were becoming life habits.

I recalled one of my first coach trainers saying, "There is a difference between *doing* coaching and *being* a coach." Coaching is not just about using skills in specific situations. As coaching gets in your bones, it's a way of being with others. The mental habits of being present, receiving instead of listening, and releasing judgment change the dynamics of relationships. Using reflective statements followed by affirming questions decreases assumptions, keeping the conversation on the same page.

Clearly, my friends felt seen. Our connections deepened. My presence made a difference in our relationships. I realized I was on my way to being a coach.

BEING A COACH

If you are new to coaching, don't wait until you feel confident to practice. Herminia Ibarra, professor of organizational behavior at INSEAD and Harvard, said we cannot develop ourselves by planning what to do in the future when we have more money and prestige. She said we need to start today by making small adjustments in our behavior because we are defined by "the things we do, the company we keep, and the stories we tell about our work and lives."[1] When people ask what you do, proudly tell them you are a coach. Whenever you have permission, engage others with coaching. When you witness the impact you have in helping people resolve dilemmas and move forward, you will begin to define yourself differently. Then, as your identity shifts, you move from practicing coaching to being a coach in all your interactions—face-to-face, on online platforms, in meetings, in hallways, and in your lunch conversations.

> When you are *being* a coach, people feel seen, heard, and valued. Acknowledge your impact so it becomes a part of your identity.

I wrote this book with the intention to demystify coaching for anyone wanting to have more meaningful conversations in all situations. I believe coaching keeps hope alive even in the most difficult times. We may not save the world. We may not even fix the forces that divide and cause harm. But we can inspire optimism and the will to move toward a vision of a better tomorrow when we give each other the gift of coaching.

BEING A COACHING CULTURE

In chapter 1, I described the influence coaching has on the brain to expand perceptions, help us see new possibilities, and inspire behavioral change. Whether you are the CEO or leader who champions coaching, consider bringing coaching into your organization. A look at the research done in companies teaching coaching skills to leaders has proven the power of coaching to improve productivity, engagement, and results.[2]

The number one reported benefit when organizations invest in building a coaching culture is increased employee engagement.[3] Increased engagement produces many positive outcomes, including decreased absenteeism, lower turnover, and quicker adaptation to change.[4] Organizations that commit to building coaching cultures provide coaching for senior leaders, train managers to use coaching skills, and encourage employees at all levels to seek coaching from managers and mentors to reach their goals.

A leader in one of my coaching classes in Kenya said, "You gave me a new dimension and techniques I have practiced ever since your program. As a result, I see the development of more leaders in our organization plus a higher level of service, improved staff morale, and commitment of heart and energy."

> Being a coach in an organization calls forth courage and the will to act. If coaching is widespread, you will have a connected, courageous culture.

A senior leader for a global shipping company said, "Every day I feel I am getting stronger in choosing the right words and forming the right questions. I understand others at a much deeper level. The results are impressive."

Most companies start by teaching coaching skills to some of their leaders. I believe getting support from senior leaders to integrate the skills after the training is vital. Managers need to feel supported so they will take the time to regularly practice coaching until the skills feel like a natural part of their conversations.

When I teach coaching skills to leaders, I ask the CEO, or other senior leader if the CEO is not available, to open the session. These leaders often speak of their own powerful experiences of being coached. Many times, they've stayed all day.

Before delivering training programs, I strategize with the internal sponsors of the program about how to measure results so they have evidence that will inspire the entire organization to embrace coaching. Some of my clients have created short videos to share with all employees, even factory workers, featuring what they will gain when their leaders use a coaching approach in their conversations. Please reach out to me if you want examples of organizations that have worked toward being a coaching culture.

> When you create cultures that foster the safety to fully express oneself in conversations, you not only bring out the best in people but bring out the best in yourself.

At the beginning of my classes I ask leaders what they will be remembered for after they move on. At the end of the program, I ask the same question. Their answers change. Learning how to hold meaningful conversations with coaching changes lives in ways we all want to be remembered for.

COACHING MAKES A DIFFERENCE

Looking back now over the twenty-five years I've been coaching, I am grateful for being able to hang out with coaches around the world. I still enjoy being with old friends, but I feel most at home with coaches who are passionate about the differences we are making with coaching.

In our divided, disconnected world, coaching brings people together. When people are overwhelmed, stressed, and angry, coaching reminds them of their purpose, visions, and power to move forward. Coaching gives hope to their desires. With just one reflection and one question, coaching can expand who they think they are and what they can do with their one, valuable life.

I applaud you for doing the exercises in this book no matter how you planned to use coaching when you opened the book to the first page. I am grateful for your commitment to find your way to these last pages. As Margaret Wheatley says, you are "a warrior of the human spirit."[5] Thank you.

NOTES

INTRODUCTION

1. From this point forward, the word *coach* refers to anyone using the skills and abilities described in this book, whether you are a professional coach, you are an internal coach or leader in a company, or you use a coaching approach to your conversations. The word *client* refers to the person being coached. Clients include people who don't pay for coaching such as employees and peers.

PART I

1. International Coaching Federation, "Core Competencies," accessed December 13, 2019, http://coachfederation.org/core-competencies.
2. Alfred Adler, *Social Interest: Adler's Key to the Meaning of Life* (Oxford: Oneworld, 1998), v.
3. Adler, *Social Interest*.
4. John Dewey, *How We Think* (Boston: D. C. Heath, 1910), 51.
5. Dewey, *How We Think*, 9.

CHAPTER 1

1. International Coach Federation, "Global Consumer Awareness Study," 2017, https://coachfederation.org/research/consumer-awareness-study.
2. Lesley Fair, "Business 'Coaches' Ejected from the Game—for Life," Consumer Information, Federal Trade Commission, Division of Consumer and Business Education, February 14, 2019.
3. Daniel Kahneman, *Thinking, Fast and Slow* (New York: Farrar, Straus and Giroux, 2011). Kahneman describes our lazy brains and what happens when thinking is disrupted externally on pages 24, 33, 51, 89, 174.
4. Maria Popova, "How We Think: John Dewey on the Art of Reflection and Fruitful Curiosity in an Age of Instant Opinions and Information Overload," Brain Pickings, https://www.brainpickings.org/2014/08/18/how-we-think-john-dewey/.
5. Hal Gregersen, "Bursting the CEO Bubble," *Harvard Business Review*, March–April 2017, 76–83.

6. Michael Gazzaniga, *Who's in Charge? Free Will and the Science of the Brain* (New York: Ecco, 2011), 43.

7. Sheila Heen and Douglas Stone, "Find the Coaching in Criticism," *Harvard Business Review*, January–February 2014, https://hbr .org/2014/01/find-the-coaching-in-criticism.

8. Marcia Reynolds, *The Discomfort Zone: How Leaders Turn Difficult Conversations into Breakthroughs* (San Francisco: Berrett-Koehler, 2014), 3–4.

9. Monika Hamori, Jie Cao, and Burak Koyuncu, "Why Top Young Managers Are in a Nonstop Job Hunt," *Harvard Business Review*, July–August 2012, http://hbr.org/2012/07/ why-top-young -managers-are-in-a-nonstop-job-hunt/.

CHAPTER 2

1. Richard Boyatzis, Melvin Smith, and Ellen Van Oosten, *Helping People Change: Coaching with Compassion for Lifelong Learning and Growth* (Boston: Harvard Business Review Press, 2019).

PART II

1. Michael S. Gazzaniga, *Who's in Charge? Free Will and the Science of the Brain* (New York: Ecco, 2011), 136.

CHAPTER 3

1. Paul Murray, *The Mark and the Void* (New York: Farrar, Straus and Giroux, 2015), 365.

CHAPTER 4

1. Richard J. Davidson and Sharon Begley, *The Emotional Life of Your Brain: How Its Unique Patterns Affect the Way You Think, Feel, and Live—and How You Can Change Them* (New York: Penguin, 2012), 60.

2. Agata Blaszczak-Boxe, "Too Much Emotional Intelligence Is a Bad Thing," *Scientific American Mind*, March 1, 2017, 83.

3. Ron Carucci, "4 Ways to Get Honest, Critical Feedback from Your Employees," *Harvard Business Review*, November 23, 2017, https:// hbr.org/2017/11/4-ways-to-get-honest-critical-feedback-from- your-employees.

CHAPTER 5

1. Hannah Arendt, *The Life of the Mind* (New York: Harcourt Brace Jovanovich, 1978), 15.

2. Jonathan Gottschall, "Storytelling Animals: 10 Surprising Ways That Story Dominates Our Lives," *The Blog*, HuffPost, updated June 21, 2012, https://www.huffpost.com/entry/humans-story-telling_b_1440917.

3. Bertram Gawronski, "Six Lessons for a Cogent Science of Implicit Bias and Its Criticism," *Perspectives on Psychological Science* 14, no. 4 (2019): 574–595.

4. Eli Saslow, "The White Flight of Derek Black," *Washington Post*, October 15, 2016.

5. Warren Berger, *A More Beautiful Question: The Power of Inquiry to Spark Breakthrough Ideas* (New York: Bloomsbury, 2014), 58.

6. John Dewey, *How We Think* (Boston: D.C. Heath, 1910), 11.

7. Marcia Reynolds, *Outsmart Your Brain: How to Master Your Mind When Emotions Take the Wheel*, 2nd ed. (Phoenix: Covisioning, 2017), 80–81.

8. A. H. Almaas, *The Unfolding Now: Realizing Your True Nature through the Practice of Presence* (Boston: Shambhala, 2008), 187.

CHAPTER 6

1. Siyuan Liu et al., "Neural Correlates of Lyrical Improvisation: An fMRI Study of Freestyle Rap," *Scientific Reports* 2, no. 834 (2012).

2. Dori Meinert, "Brené Brown: Drop the Armor, Dare to Lead," SHRM, June 24, 2019, https://www.shrm.org/hr-today/news/hr -news/Pages/Brene-Brown-Drop-the-Armor-Dare-to-Lead.aspx.

CHAPTER 7

1. John Renesch, "A Mature Approach to Commitment," *Mini-Keynote Editorials* (blog), June 2019, http://renesch.com/2019/a-mature -approach-to-commitment/.

PART III

1. Doug Silsbee, *Presence-Based Coaching* (San Francisco: Jossey-Bass, 2008), 2.

2. Rollin McCraty, *The Energetic Heart: Bioelectromagnetic Interactions within and between People* (Boulder Creek, CA: HeartMath Institute, 2003).

3. Carl Jung, *Modern Man in Search of a Soul*, trans. W. S. Dell and Cary F. Baynes (London: Routledge Press, 2001), 49.

4. Daniel Goleman, *Social Intelligence: The New Science of Human Relationships* (New York: Bantam, 2006), 275.

5. William A. Kahn, "Psychological Conditions of Personal Engagement and Disengagement at Work," *Academy of Management Journal* 33, no. 4 (2017): 708.

6. Marcia Reynolds, *The Discomfort Zone: How Leaders Turn Difficult Conversations into Breakthroughs* (San Francisco: Berrett-Koehler, 2014), 27.

7. Shari M. Gellar and Stephen W. Porges, "Therapeutic Presence: Neurophysiological Mechanisms Mediating Feeling Safe in Therapeutic Relationships," *Journal of Psychotherapy Integration* 24, no. 3 (2014): 178–192.

CHAPTER 8

1. Kenneth Nowack, "Facilitating Successful Behavioral Change: Beyond Goal Setting to Goal Flourishing," *Consulting Psychology Journal* 69, no. 3 (2017): 153–171.

2. Michael Murphy and Rhea White, *In the Zone: Transcendent Experience in Sports* (New York: Penguin, 1995).

3. Mihaly Csikszentmihalyi, *Flow: The Psychology of Optimal Experience* (New York: Harper and Row, 1990), 24.

4. Marcia Reynolds, *Outsmart Your Brain: How to Master Your Mind When Emotions Take the Wheel* (Phoenix: Covisioning, 2017), 44–54.

5. Johann Hari, "Everything You Think You Know about Addiction Is Wrong," TEDGlobalLondon, June 2015, https://www.ted.com/talks/johann_hari_everything_you_think_you_know_about_addiction_is_wrong.

CHAPTER 9

1. Julian Treasure, "5 Ways to Listen Better," TEDGlobal, July 2011, https://www.ted.com/talks/julian_treasure_5_ways_to_listen_better.

2. Alice Park, "Emotions May Not Be So Universal After All," *Time*, March 6, 2014, https://time.com/14478/emotions-may-not-be-so-universal-after-all/.

3. Grant Soosalu and Marvin Oka, "Neuroscience and the Three Brains of Leadership," mBraining, 2012, https://www.mbraining.com/mbit-and-Leadership.

4. Shaun Gallagher et al., *The Neurophenomenology of Awe and Wonder: Towards a Non-reductionist Cognitive Science* (Basingstoke, UK: Palgrave Macmillan, 2015), 22–23.

5. Daniel J. Siegel, *The Developing Mind: How Relationships and the Brain Interact to Shape Who We Are*, 2nd ed. (New York: Guilford Press, 2012).

6. A. H. Almaas, *Spacecruiser Inquiry: True Guidance for the Inner Journey* (Boston: Shambhala, 2002), 321.

CHAPTER 10

1. Paul Rozin and Edward B. Royzman, "Negativity Bias, Negativity Dominance, and Contagion," *Personality and Social Psychology Review* 5, no. 4 (2001): 296–320.

2. Howard J. Ross, *Everyday Bias: Identifying and Navigating Unconscious Judgments in Our Daily Lives* (Lanham, MD: Rowman & Littlefield, 2014).

3. Margaret S. Clark, Rebecca L. Dyer, and John A. Bargh. "Revealed: Why We Cry When We Are Happy," Yale University Study, Biospace.com, November 13, 2014, https://www.biospace.com/article /revealed-why-we-cry-when-we-are-happy-yale-university-study-/.

4. Will Sharon, "Hesitation on the Hero's Journey," YouTube video, July 22, 2019, https://www.youtube.com/watch?v=P-pAwqzymqE&.

WRAP-UP

1. Herminia Ibarra, *Working Identity: Unconventional Strategies for Reinventing Your Career* (Boston: Harvard Business School Press, 2003), xi.

2. Joel A. DiGirolamo and J. Thomas Tkach, "An Exploration of Managers and Leaders Using Coaching Skills," *Consulting Psychology Journal* 71, no. 3 (2019), https://psycnet.apa.org/record/2019-23918-001.

3. Jenna Filipkowski, *Building a Coaching Culture*, Human Capital Institute, October 1, 2014, http://www.hci.org/hr-research /building-coaching-culture.

4. Jenna Filipkowski, Mark Ruth, and Abby Heverin, *Building a Coaching Culture for Change Management*, Human Capital Institute and International Coaching Federation, September 25, 2018, http://www .hci.org/hr-research/building-coaching-culture-change-management.

5. Margaret J. Wheatley, *Who Do We Choose to Be? Facing Reality, Claiming Leadership, Restoring Sanity* (Oakland: Berrett-Koehler, 2017), 253–266.

ACKNOWLEDGMENTS

THIS BOOK IS the product of all the coaches, clients, mentors, teachers, and friends who have been in my life since I found an article on coaching twenty-five years ago. You may not be named here, but know I am thankful beyond words for our paths crossing. I am lucky to know you.

Many thanks to Neal Maillet, my editor, for having the courage to challenge me when my ideas are cloudy, even though he doesn't need courage for me to hear his wisdom—and the truth.

I am in awe of my vast global coaching community for the friendships and the learning I receive from my colleagues. I especially want to thank DJ Mitsch, president of the Pyramid Resource Group, for having the courage and foresight to found the Healthcare Coaching Institute and appoint me the training director. Designing and delivering the training for the program helped me write this book. I learn so much every time I teach.

Thanks also to Zoran Todorovic, Tess He, Allow Sui, and Svetlana Chumakova for trusting me to teach coaching for your schools and to add and change my classes frequently as I keep learning how to master coaching.

Most recently, I am so appreciative of my partnership with Dorothy Siminovitch, who constantly shifts and deepens my view of mastery.

To my cheerleaders—Teri-E Belf and Vickie Sullivan—you are both consistent sources of support. Thanks to Hayley Foster, Wendy White, Linda Lunden, Eileen McDargh, Dennece McKelvy, Stephanie Rosol, and Diana Groh for your amazing minds and helpful ideas. Special thanks to Toni Koch, who keeps my life sane while I am running around the world.

I am grateful for all my students and clients. This book is about what I learned from you.

Above all, I am grateful with all my heart for Karl Schnell, my life partner. He unconditionally supports me and my work, always making sure I have the space I need even when it impacts our plans. Without him, my life would not be whole.

INDEX

Page references followed by *fig* indicate a figure.

ABOUT THE AUTHOR

Marcia Reynolds, PsyD, Master Certified Coach

WHAT DOES IT take to influence others to change their lives for the better? That is the question Dr. Marcia Reynolds has been asking for three decades. She knew telling people what is best for them doesn't work, even though she turned her life around before nearly destroying it as a teenager. She found her answer when she discovered coaching. She has since devoted her work to understanding the science of coaching—why it is so powerful in shifting people's minds and behaviors and what the best ways are to effectively coach. She is passionate about teaching what she learns to coaches and leaders around the world. She knows coaching can bring people together in a respectful, caring way that makes our world a better place to live in for all.

As president of Covisioning LLC, Marcia coaches executives and teaches coaching skills to students and leaders, working in forty-one countries to date. She also consults with change agents who want to establish coaching cultures in their organizations. She is a frequent speaker at conferences and has presented at the Harvard Kennedy School and Cornell University as well as universities in Europe and Asia.

Marcia is a pioneer in the coaching profession. She was the fifth global president of the International Coach Federation (which became the International Coaching Federation in 2020) and was recently inducted into its Circle of Distinction for her many years of service to the global coaching community. Currently, she is the training director for the Healthcare Coaching Institute and is also on the faculty for the International Coaching Academy in Russia and Create China Coaching in China. She also teaches coaching skills classes in organizations around the world. She is recognized by Global Gurus as one of the top five coaches in the world.

Before she launched her own business, her greatest success came from designing the employee development program for a global semiconductor company facing bankruptcy. Within three years, the company turned around and became the number one stock market success in 1993.

Interviews and excerpts from her books *The Discomfort Zone: How Leaders Turn Difficult Conversations into Breakthroughs; Outsmart Your Brain: How to Master Your Mind When Emotions Take the Wheel;* and *Wander Woman: How High-Achieving Women Find Contentment and Direction* have appeared in many places, including *Fast Company,* Forbes.com, CNN.com, *Psychology Today,* the *Globe and Mail,* and the *Wall Street Journal,* and she has appeared in business magazines in Europe and Asia and on *ABC World News.*

Marcia is passionate about evoking transformation with coaching. Email or call her if you or others in your organization have a need that coaching can meet or you want to teach your leaders or coaches to have more transformational conversations: Marcia@covisioning.com or +1-602-954-9030. Her website is https://covisioning.com/.

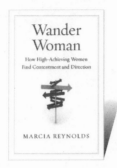